D1301399

WHAT IS TERRORISM?

WHAT IS TERRORISM?

Leonard Weinberg
and
William L. Eubank
University of Nevada, Reno

Series Consulting Editors

Leonard Weinberg and William L. Eubank
University of Nevada, Reno

CHELSEA HOUSE
P U B L I S H E R S
An imprint of Infobase Publishing

What Is Terrorism?

Chelsea House
An imprint of Infobase Publishing
132 West 31st Street
New York NY 10001

Library of Congress Cataloging-in-Publication Data

Weinberg, Leonard, 1939–
   What is terrorism?/Leonard Weinberg and William L. Eubank.
     p. cm. —(The roots of terrorism)
   Includes bibliographical references and index.
ISBN 0-7910-8305-5 (hard cover)
 1. Terrorism—History—Juvenile literature. I. Eubank, William Lee.
II. Title. III. Series.
HV6431.W443 2005
303.6'25—dc22   2005027569

Series and cover design by Takeshi Takahashi

Printed in the United States of America

Bang 21C 10 9 8 7 6 5 4 3 2 1

This book is printed on acid-free paper.

TABLE OF CONTENTS

INTRODUCTION

Leonard Weinberg and William L. Eubank
University of Nevada, Reno

Terrorism is hard to ignore. Almost every day television news shows, newspapers, magazines, and Websites run and re-run pictures of dramatic and usually bloody acts of violence carried out by ferocious-looking terrorists or claimed by shadowy militant groups. It is often hard not to be scared when we see people like us killed or maimed by terrorist attacks at fast food restaurants, in office buildings, on public buses and trains, or along normal-looking streets.

This kind of fear is exactly what those staging terrorist attacks hope to achieve. They want the public, especially the American public, to feel a profound sense of fear. Often the leaders of terrorist groups want the public not only frightened by the attack, but also angry at the government because it seems unable to protect them from these violent assaults.

This series of books for young people has two related purposes. The first is to place the events we see in context. We want young readers to know what terrorism is about: Who its perpetrators are, where they come from, and what they hope to gain by their violence. We also want to answer some basic questions about this type of violence: What is terrorism? What do we mean when we use the term? Is one man's terrorist another man's freedom fighter? Is terrorism new, a kind of asymmetrical warfare just invented at the beginning of the twenty-first century? Or, does terrorism have a long history stretching back over the centuries? Does terrorism ever end? Should we expect to face waves of terrorist violence stretching into the indefinite future?

This series' second purpose is to reduce the anxieties and fears of young readers. Getting a realistic picture of what terrorism is all about, knowing what is true and what is not true about it helps us "get a grip." Young readers will learn, we hope, what constitutes realistic concerns about the danger of terrorism versus irrational fear. By understanding the nature of the threat, we help defeat one of the terrorists' basic aims: spreading terror.

The first volume in the series, *What is Terrorism?*, by Leonard Weinberg and William L. Eubank, begins by defining the term "terrorism," then goes on to explain the immediate aims and long-term objectives of those who decide to use this unconventional form of violence. Weinberg and Eubank point out that terrorism did not begin with the 9/11 attacks on the United States. In fact, terrorist violence has a long history, one the authors trace from its religious roots in the ancient Middle East up to current times.

For those who believe that terrorist campaigns, once started, are endless, Jeffrey Ian Ross's *Will Terrorism End?* will come as a useful antidote. Ross calls our attention to the various ways in which terrorist episodes have ended in the past. Many readers will be surprised to learn that most of the terrorist organizations that were active in Latin America, Western Europe, and the United States just a few decades ago have passed from the scene. For example, the Irish Republican Army (IRA), long active in paramilitary operations in Northern Ireland, is now in the process of turning to peaceful political participation.

Between accounts of the beginning and end of terrorism are books that approach the problem in two different ways. Dipak K. Gupta (*Who are the Terrorists?*) and Assaf Moghadam (*The Roots of Terrorism*) answer general questions about the origins of terrorists and terrorist organizations. Gupta provides profiles of individual terrorists and terrorist groups, in addition to exploring the issues that inspire terrorists. Moghadam, on the other hand, is more concerned with the organizational and social roots of terrorism. For example: What causes people to join terrorist groups? What are the grievances that often give rise to terrorist campaigns?

While Gupta and Moghadam examine the roots of terrorism in general terms, Jack Levin and Arie Perliger's books each have a specific geographic focus. Levin's *Domestic Terrorism* brings the story close to home by describing domestic terrorist activity in the United States over the last half century. Perliger's book, *Middle Eastern Terrorism*, offers an account of terrorist activity in the region of the world with which such violence is most closely identified.

Finally, we believe that young readers will come away from this series of books with a much clearer understanding of what terrorism is and what those individuals and groups who carry out terrorist attacks are like. ■

CHAPTER 1

CONFRONTING TERRORISM

October 23, 1983—Simultaneous suicide truck-bomb attacks are made on American and French compounds in Beirut, Lebanon. A 12,000-pound bomb destroys the U.S. compound, killing 242 Americans; 58 French troops are killed when a 400-pound device destroys a French base. Islamic Jihad claims responsibility.

February 26, 1993—The World Trade Center in New York City is badly damaged when a car bomb planted by Islamic terrorists explodes in an underground garage. The bomb leaves 6 people dead and 1,000 injured. The men who carry out the attack are followers of Umar Abd al-Rahman, an Egyptian cleric who preached in the New York City area at the time.

1

March 20, 1995—Twelve people are killed and 5,700 injured in a sarin (nerve gas) attack on a crowded subway station in the center of Tokyo, Japan. A similar attack occurs nearly simultaneously in the Yokohama subway system. The Aum Shinrikyo cult is blamed for the attacks.

April 19, 1995—Right-wing extremists Timothy McVeigh and Terry Nichols destroy the Alfred P. Murrah Federal Building in Oklahoma City with a massive truck bomb that kills 166 and injures hundreds more, in what was at that point the largest terrorist attack on American soil.

September 11, 2001—Two hijacked airliners crash into the Twin Towers of the World Trade Center. Soon after, the Pentagon is struck by a third hijacked plane. A fourth hijacked plane, suspected to be bound for a high-profile target in Washington, D.C., crashes into a field in southern Pennsylvania. The attacks kill 3,025 U.S. citizens and other nationals. President Bush and Cabinet officials indicate that Osama bin Laden is the prime suspect and that they consider the United States to be in a state of war with international terrorism. In the aftermath of the attacks, the United States forms the Global Coalition Against Terrorism.

DEFINING TERRORISM

What do all these events, as reported by the U.S. State Department,[1] have in common? Students and their teachers would agree that all of these violent attacks are acts of terrorism. What exactly makes them acts of terrorism: The violence itself? The fact that most of the people killed or injured were not soldiers ready for battle but civilians going about their daily lives? Do we use the term *terrorism* because the violence occurred in places where it is unexpected: in theaters, outside shopping centers, on buses and planes, in subway stations?

Some attention should be given to the persons responsible for perpetrating the violence. Did they carry out the attacks because they hated the particular individuals they killed or injured? In most cases, the answer is "no." In fact, for the most part, the victims were perfect strangers, individuals with whom the perpetrators had no previous contact. Maybe the motive was greed: They killed to make a profit. Still another possibility is that the killers, some of whom committed suicide in the course of carrying out their attacks, were simply crazy. Why else would someone wish to kill large numbers of perfect strangers if he or she were not suffering from some type of mental disturbance?

In answering these questions, let us first consider the matter of motive. Why did they do it? The answer is that, in all the events recounted in this chapter, the attackers had a political motive: They were acting on behalf of a political cause. Sometimes the cause was nationalist: independence from Russia for Chechnya or separation of Northern Ireland from Great Britain. Sometimes the cause involved a complex set of grievances against the American government or Americans more generally, as was the case in the Oklahoma City bombing or the World Trade Center attacks. These attackers were not acting out of some private motivation. The perpetrators all had a political agenda that they believed would be helped by staging these attacks.

Publicity and psychology are at the heart of terrorism. The attacks mentioned previously all received extensive publicity, especially from television networks. If the attack is dramatic enough or kills enough people, as the 9/11 attacks on the World Trade Center and the Pentagon did, television viewers all over the world will very quickly become aware of what happened. In fact, terrorism is a kind of politically motivated violence in which publicity—sending a message—plays a crucial role. Peter Kropotkin, a nineteenth-century anarchist, referred to terrorism as "propaganda by deed," a means by which small groups can attract attention to a political cause, no matter what the cause may be. In the United States, the law defines terrorism as

"... premeditated, politically motivated violence perpetrated against noncombatant targets by subnational groups or clandestine agents, usually intended to influence an audience ..."[2]

Terrorism, then, is a tactic, a particularly violent form of political communication that depends heavily on modern means of communication, such as television and the Internet, to send a message to some audience in the hope that it will affect their emotions and change their behavior. What do terrorists hope to achieve by their violence?

Other Major Terrorist Events

June 23, 1985—A bomb destroys an Air India jet over the Atlantic Ocean, killing 329 people on board. Both Sikh and Kashmiri terrorists are blamed for the attack. Two cargo handlers are killed at the Tokyo Airport in Japan when another Sikh bomb explodes in an Air Canada aircraft en route to India.

May 21, 1991—A female member of the LTTE (Liberation Tigers of Tamil Eelam) kills herself, Prime Minister Rajiv Gandhi, and 16 others by detonating an explosive vest after presenting a garland of flowers to the former prime minister during an election rally in the Indian state of Tamil Nadu.

February 26, 1996—In Jerusalem, a suicide bomber blows up a bus, killing 26 people, including 3 U.S. citizens, and injuring 80 people, including 3 more U.S. citizens.

November 17, 1997—Al-Gama'at al-Islamiyya (IG) gunmen shoot and kill 58 tourists and 4 Egyptians and wound 26 others at the Hatshepsut Temple in the Valley of the Kings near Luxor. Thirty-four Swiss, eight Japanese, five Germans, four Britons, one French, one Colombian, one dual Bulgarian/British citizen, and nine Egyptians are among the wounded.

Terrorist attacks not a new phenomenon in Europe

Terror experts say Thursday's four coordinated attacks on London's subway and bus systems have "all the trademarks of the al-Qaida network." The attacks came on the opening day of the G-8 summit in Gleneagles, Scotland, and a day after the city was awarded the 2012 Olympics.

Major attacks in Europe since 1996

1996	1997	1998	1999	2000	2001	2002	2003	2004	2005

Sept. 11 attacks (U.S.)

	Dec. 3, 1996	Aug. 15, 1998	June 8, 2000	March 4, 2001	March 9, 2001	March 11, 2004	July 7, 2005
Place	Paris	Omagh, Ireland	Athens, Greece	London	Hernani, Spain	Madrid, Spain	London
Target(s)	Subway train bombing	Car bombing at local courthouse	British Defense Attache assassination	Car bombing at BBC studios	Car bombing of police	Explosions at three train stations	Blasts at three train stations, bus
Killed	Four	29	One	One	Two	191	At least 40
Injured	86	330				1,500	700
Group responsible	Algerian extremists suspected	Real IRA	17 November (revolutionary organization)	Real IRA	Basque Fatherland and Liberty (ETA)	Islamic militants	Al-Qaida suspected

SOURCE: Department of State   AP

The July 7, 2005, terrorist bombings in London may have been shocking, but they were not entirely unusual. This graphic lays out the terrorist attacks that have taken place in Europe since 1996.

TERRORISM AS A TACTIC: THE IMMEDIATE BENEFITS

Communist leader V.I. Lenin (1870–1924) once observed that the purpose of terrorism was to terrify. Clearly, one purpose behind campaigns of terrorist violence is to terrify various audiences, to leave people with the impression that they are not safe and that anything can happen at any time. After the 9/11 attacks, for example, many residents of New York City had the feeling that they might face death simply in following their daily routines. If members of the public are panicked and feel vulnerable, they often turn to the government in the belief that guaranteeing the protection of physical safety is the government's responsibility. If the government cannot perform this function, the public may very well lose confidence in it—often precisely the effect the terrorists hoped to achieve.

Loss of confidence can have very tangible consequences. Here is an example: On November 17, 1997 (see sidebar: *Other Major Terrorist Events* on page 4), members of the IG shot and killed 58 foreign tourists (some victims had their throats slashed as well) while they were visiting the Valley of the Kings, an ancient site in Lower Egypt. Egypt earns a lot of money from its tourism industry. Over the next few years, tourism in the country suffered a significant decline as thousands of would-be vacationers refused to visit out of fear that their lives might be in danger.

Spreading fear is not the only effect that terrorist violence may have. Another is, of course, the achievement of publicity. By carrying out dramatic acts of violence, terrorists call attention to causes and issues with which not many people were familiar beforehand. In the absence of a terrorist campaign, relatively few Americans would be aware of the existence of secessionist movements such as those in Indian-ruled Kashmir and on the island nation of Sri Lanka. Terrorism compels attention more than long-winded speeches and propaganda pamphlets can.

Terrorism can also be aimed at provoking the authorities into an overreaction. Like the martial art of jujitsu, in which one contestant often uses his opponent's own strength to defeat him, terrorist groups may use a government's power to help achieve their own goals and objectives. If an act of terrorism can provoke a government into carrying out indiscriminate attacks against the part of the population that a terrorist group claims to lead, it may antagonize people who belong to that population so that they come to sympathize with the group. In this way, the government may, in effect, do the work of the terrorist group for it.

From 1834 to 1962, the North African state of Algeria was a colony under French rule. During the 1950s, Muslim rebels sought to force France to abandon its colonial control. The rebels, a comparative handful of the majority Muslim population, carried out a series of terrorist attacks on Algeria's European settlers. The French government responded to the outraged settlers and cracked down on the country's Muslims, rebel or not, particularly in the big cities. By targeting the entire non-European population, rather than focusing on the guerrillas, the French unintentionally did the work of the rebels for them. Most Algerians came to see the government as a hated enemy by the end of the conflict, which resulted in the achievement of Algerian independence in 1962.

These are reactions or potential reactions of audiences likely to be hostile to the aims and objectives of those carrying out terrorist attacks. It is clear, however, that these attacks may be carried out in order to have an impact on audiences likely to be sympathetic to those who commit them. If acts of terrorism may be seen as retaliation for injuries suffered by a particular group, members of the group may feel that they have been avenged by the terrorists. Indian prime minister Indira Gandhi was assassinated by members of her Sikh bodyguard in 1984. In India, where the Sikh religion developed, Sikhs are a minority group whose population is centered in the state of Punjab. Many Sikhs in the Punjab and other parts of the world expressed delight with the prime minister's assassination because they regarded Gandhi as responsible for the deaths of many coreligionists during an invasion of a Sikh holy place that she had ordered.

Terrorist attacks may also raise the morale of people in the population who feel helpless in the face of what they regard as an unjust or repressive government or foreign occupation. One of the aims of the suicide bombings directed against American troops and other foreigners in Iraq following the military occupation in 2003 has been to show ordinary Iraqis, especially members of the Sunni branch of Islam, that the foreign forces are not all-powerful. They, too, can be targeted for lethal levels of force. Many ordinary Iraqis may have their morale raised as a result. The same may be said about the intent of the suicide bombing campaign conducted by various Palestinian groups against Israelis since the beginning of the al-Aqsa Intifada in fall 2000.

Those who commit acts of terrorism certainly have an immediate purpose. Most of the major ones, including spreading fear, creating publicity for the group's cause, provoking the authorities into overreacting, retaliating against an enemy, and raising the morale of people the terrorist group hopes to lead, were addressed in the previous paragraphs. Perpetrators of violence usually have long-term goals that they hope to achieve as well. Bearing in mind that terrorism is simply a tactic that may be used by groups with different political agendas, the question becomes, "What are these goals?"

LONG-TERM GOALS OF TERRORISTS

What are the long-term objectives of those who wage campaigns of terror? One that is often mentioned involves starting a social revolution. In Latin America especially, terrorist organizations have historically hoped that their violent activities would ignite a popular revolution by peasant farmers and urban slum dwellers to overthrow the existing government and replace it with a socialist regime. In Peru, a group known as the Sendero Luminoso (Shining Path) employs a combination of urban terrorism and rural guerrilla warfare in its campaign to bring down the elected government in Lima. Likewise, in Colombia, the Revolutionary Armed Forces of Colombia's leaders share this goal and employ kidnapping for ransom, as well as the Shining Path's tactics, in a long-term struggle to topple the government in Bogotá.

Far more common these days are organizations that use terrorism in the hope of achieving a nationalist or separatist goal. They either hope to create a new, independent country in a territory that previously was part of another one, or they want to detach some region of one country and merge it with another. Here are some examples:

Tamil Tigers march on the road to Thopigila Camp, their main military base in eastern Sri Lanka. The Tamil Tigers have been fighting the majority government since the 1980s in the hope of someday establishing their own separate state.

In Sri Lanka, the island nation located off the southeast coast of India, there is an ethnic group called the Tamils. Many Tamils feel that they have been the target of discrimination by the government in Colombo (the capital of Sri Lanka), a government dominated by the majority Sinhalese ethnic group. To make matters worse, there is a religious element to the conflict. The Tamils are Hindu, whereas the Sinhalese are Buddhist. These religious differences have strained Tamil–Sinhalese relations. Since the 1980s, an organization known as the Liberation Tigers of Tamil Eelam (LTTE) has waged a terrorist campaign, including suicide bombings, in an effort to create an independent state for the Tamils in the northeastern part of the country. Thousands of Sri Lankans have died along the way.

The Basques live in the northern regions of Spain and the southern parts of France. They possess a unique language and culture. Many Basques, particularly those in Spain, wish to achieve a separate national identity despite the fact that the Basque region already enjoys a significant amount of local self-government. For some, local control does not go far enough: They want complete national independence. Among those who feel this way are members of Euskadi Ta Askatasuna (Basque Homeland and Freedom, or ETA), a terrorist band that killed approximately 850 Spaniards all over the country between the 1960s and 2005—so far without achieving their ultimate objective.[3]

Religious goals and objectives have been important motives for terrorist acts, especially in recent years. Sometimes, as in the case of the state of Kashmir in India or on the island of Mindanao in the Philippines, the goals of those who stage terrorist attacks are a mix of ethnic and religious objectives. In these particular cases, the groups that carry out the attacks have nationalist goals. They want Kashmir to be detached from India in order to become part of Pakistan and to separate Mindanao from the government in Manila, respectively. In addition to these nationalist aims, there is a very strong religious element in both cases. The groups involved are Islamists or Islamic fundamentalists who define themselves as engaged in a "holy war" to transform these territories into part of a worldwide Muslim community (*umma*) and thereby fulfill their obligations to God.

Terrorism inspired by religious goals is by no means confined to Muslims or the Muslim world for that matter. In recent decades, Sikh groups in the Punjab section of India; Jewish settlers who live on the West Bank (in territory Israel occupied during the 1967 war); and extremist Christians who hope to accelerate the coming of the Millennium (the thousand-year period before the "second coming" of Christ and the final struggle between good and evil); have all carried out terrorist attacks in order to further their goals.

Sometimes violent organizations use terrorism to prevent changes that they believe threaten their own concerns and interests. In the United States during the 1950s and 1960s, members of the Ku Klux Klan used terrorist tactics in the South to stop African Americans from exercising their right to vote and to prevent racial integration of schools and other public facilities. In Latin American countries such as Colombia, it is not uncommon for wealthy landowners to hire and organize violent paramilitary gangs whose goal is to prevent farm workers from receiving higher wages or better working conditions.

Single issues or single problems can also motivate outbreaks of terrorist violence. These are narrowly focused concerns such as opposition to abortion or to the use of live animals for scientific or commercial laboratory experiments. In the United States, loosely organized groups such as the Earth Liberation Front (ELF) use terrorist tactics, largely arson, in efforts to prevent logging and construction of ski lodges in environmentally sensitive areas. The Animal Liberation Front (ALF) has set fire to medical laboratories to prevent their use by researchers who conduct experiments on live animals. There have been cases in which ALF activists have "liberated" fur-bearing animals from the farms that housed them to prevent the use of their pelts for fur coats and other fashionable apparel.

Abortion is an issue that clearly excites strong feelings, at least in the United States. In most cases, the passions of abortion opponents have been channeled into conventional political activity such as lobbying efforts in the halls of Congress, public picketing of women's clinics, and appeals to the courts. In some instances, however, the opposition has become violent. Physicians and nurses who practice abortion have been murdered, and the medical facilities where the procedures are performed have been fire-bombed. In these instances, the violence is clearly terroristic in character. The perpetrators wish to terrify both those who seek and those who provide abortions in the hope that the practice will cease.

A FEW IMPORTANT DISTINCTIONS

As is evident from television stories about suicide bombings and kidnappings in Iraq, the Philippines, Indonesia, the Russian Federation, and elsewhere, not all terrorism involves attacks by people of one country against their fellow citizens. Militant Islamists from various Arab countries went to Iraq and Russia (in connection with the uprising in the republic of Chechnya) to carry out terrorist attacks in countries far from their homelands. In the Philippines, members of a local secessionist band, the Abu Sayyaf, have kidnapped Western tourists and held them for ransom as a way of raising money for and calling attention to their cause. In Indonesia, terrorists linked to the Jemaah Islamiyah organization detonated a bomb in a nightclub on the island of Bali, killing approximately 100 Australian tourists. In other cases, members of an "active service unit" of the Irish Republican Army (IRA) traveled to Germany in order to set off bombs at British targets located in the Federal Republic of Germany.

Like the 9/11 attacks in the United States, the above events are all acts of international terrorism. They are "international" because of the many national backgrounds of the perpetrators and victims of the attacks, as well as where the attacks were carried out. Domestic terrorism concerns attacks in which the perpetrators and the targets come from the same country and where the violence also takes place in that country. The April 1995 bombing of the Alfred P. Murrah Federal Building in Oklahoma City by Timothy McVeigh is an example of domestic terrorism. The bombings and retaliatory killings between members of rival Sunni and Shi'ite groups in such cities as Karachi and Bangalore in Pakistan is another.

Readers should also be aware of the different roles of states or governments. States or regimes can certainly conduct campaigns of terrorist violence against their own citizens. Think of the former Soviet Union under the dictatorship of Joseph Stalin, of Nazi Germany under the control of Adolf Hitler, and

Iraq when it was ruled by the Ba'athist dictatorship of Saddam Hussein. Far more people have been killed by governments seeking to terrify their own populations than have died at the hands of private terrorist organizations. This book, however, is not focused on this type of state terrorism.

It is important to know that some terrorist organizations are exclusively private in nature, enjoying no support from any state or government, whereas others have state sponsors willing to provide assistance. The regime of the ayatollahs in Iran, for example, has provided help to a number of Shi'ite terrorist groups over the years, the most important of which has been Hizbollah, or the "Party of God," in Lebanon. The regime of Saddam Hussein offered sanctuary and assistance to the late Palestinian terrorist chief Abu Nidal and members of his organization. Most significant of all, Afghanistan, when it was ruled by the Taliban, provided not only sanctuary but also training facilities for Osama bin Laden's worldwide al Qaeda network.

In some cases, national governments have little choice in the matter because they are too weak to maintain law and order within their countries' borders. In "failed states" such as Somalia, terrorist organizations are often able to operate freely—conduct training exercises, plan attacks, and stockpile weapons—not because the official government sponsors them but simply because they lack the ability to do anything about it.

For governments with a choice in the matter, the question becomes, "What do they gain by sponsoring terrorist groups?" One answer is that modern warfare using conventional means and conventional weapons is both expensive and dangerous. Countries have names and addresses. By directly confronting another country with the use or threat of military force, a government risks retaliation by its enemy. If the enemy is large and powerful, such a maneuver invites its own destruction. The same government may decide to use shadowy terrorist bands—whose clandestine natures become advantageous—as substitutes or surrogates. The government in question may deny involvement or responsibility when the state-sponsored terrorist group stages an attack against its enemy. The Libyan government of Colonel Muammar Qaddafi had a long history of such behavior before undergoing a change of heart in the 1990s. State sponsorship offers an inexpensive substitute for more open forms of military operations.

Most terrorist organizations active during the first decade of the twenty-first century do not receive support, moral or material, from states. After the world reaction to the 9/11 attacks on the United States and the March 11, 2004, terrorist bombings of commuter trains in Madrid, Spain, the United Nations and other international organizations have made it increasingly difficult for states to sponsor terrorist activities. Those who persist risk being labeled pariahs by the world community and being subjected to serious economic and political sanctions.

WEAPONS

The September 11, 2001, attacks on the World Trade Center's Twin Towers and the Pentagon killed approximately 3,000 people. Followers of Osama bin Laden murdered more people than Japanese aircraft did at Pearl Harbor on December 7, 1941. Moreover, the victims of the Japanese attack were U.S. naval and army personnel, but the 19 Islamic militants who took over civilian aircraft and crashed them into these three buildings killed mostly civilians. What weapons did the hijackers employ to murder so many people so quickly?

The answer seems self-evident but really is not. As everyone who has seen the horrifying videos of the event is aware, the 3,000 deaths were caused by the terrorists deliberately crashing planes loaded with highly flammable jet fuel into the buildings and by the fires and destruction that followed. The answer becomes more complicated when one questions how the terrorists were able to take control of the planes. The answer is that they used box cutters, small knives typically used to slice open cardboard boxes and available at hardware stores for less than a dollar. In other words, the 9/11 attacks were possible because the terrorists made use of the most primitive types of weapons.

Before the events of 9/11, the worst single act of terrorism on American soil occurred on April 19, 1995, when antigovernment activists Timothy McVeigh and Terry Nichols

A Declaration of War

In February 1998, the 40-year-old Saudi exile Osama bin Laden and a fugitive Egyptian, Ayman al-Zawahiri, arranged from their Afghan headquarters for an Arabic newspaper in London to publish what they termed a *fatwa*, issued in the name of a "World Islamic Front." A fatwa is normally an interpretation of Islamic law by a respected Islamic authority, but neither bin Laden, al-Zawahiri, nor the three others who signed this statement were scholars of Islamic law. Claiming that America had declared war against God and his messenger, they called for the murder of any American, anywhere on earth, as the "individual duty for every Muslim who can do it in any country in which it is possible to do it."

Three months later, when interviewed in Afghanistan by ABC-TV, bin Laden enlarged on these themes. He claimed it was more important for Muslims to kill Americans than to kill other infidels. "It is far better for anyone to kill a single American soldier than to squander his efforts on other activities," he said. Asked whether he approved of terrorism and of attacks on civilians, he replied: "We believe that the worst thieves in the world today and the worst terrorists are the Americans. Nothing could stop you except perhaps retaliation in kind. We do not differentiate between military and civilian. As far as we are concerned, they are all targets."*

———
* *The 9/11 Commission Report.* New York: W.W. Norton, 2004, p. 47.

detonated a truck-bomb in front of the Alfred P. Murrah Federal Building in Oklahoma City and killed 166 people. The bomb that McVeigh and Nichols constructed consisted of ammonium nitrate, which is a common fertilizer, and enough fuel oil to ignite it. These ingredients, like the box cutters, are also available at hardware stores throughout the United States.

Both before and after the Oklahoma City and 9/11 terrorist attacks, analysts inside and outside government repeatedly called the public's attention to the dangers of weapons of mass destruction (WMD). Fears that terrorist organizations like al Qaeda could produce or obtain chemical, biological, radiological, or even nuclear weapons now have become widespread. These fears are not based on works of science fiction and made-for-TV films. In 1995, members of a Japanese religious cult released sarin, a poison gas, in the Tokyo subway system, killing a dozen commuters. A few weeks after the 9/11 attacks, a still-unknown individual or individuals mailed letters laced with anthrax, a toxic agent, to members of Congress and the news media. Later still, video recordings captured in Afghanistan showed al Qaeda operatives conducting experiments on dogs using a poison gas. These developments certainly warrant concern: Instructions on how to make chemical and biological weapons are available on the Internet, and in some cases, the ingredients may be ordered and sent through the mail. There is also the problem of "loose nukes," an arsenal of nuclear weapons stockpiled by the former Soviet Union that may not be adequately supervised by the various states, such as Ukraine and Belarus, that became independent after the Soviet Union's collapse in 1991.

Weapons of mass destruction seem particularly dreadful— they literally fill people with dread. Being poisoned by unseen agents floating in the air or in the food and water we consume seems truly horrifying. Many people may be killed quickly in terrible ways.

The reality, however, is somewhat different. Now, as in the past, the majority of terrorist attacks are carried out by people who employ highly conventional weapons. For the most part, today's terrorists rely overwhelmingly on bombs, knives, and guns, much as their predecessors did more than 100 years ago, when modern terrorism first attracted the public's attention in Europe and the United States. Box cutters and ammonium nitrate are not WMD as conventionally defined, but they were used to kill thousands. Chemical and biological agents and radioactive devices may become the weapons of choice for the terrorists of the future. In the present, most terrorist attacks are carried out by individuals who use weapons normally on sale at the local Wal-Mart or Home Depot.

SUMMARY

This chapter has addressed some fundamental ideas about the nature of modern terrorism. Foremost is the definition of this violent and politically motivated activity that stresses the concept of "propaganda by deed." Terrorism is a way to send a message through the mass media to different audiences. What are the intended purposes behind these messages and what effects did the terrorists hope to achieve by sending them? What are the long-term goals of groups and organizations that carry out terrorist attacks—social revolution, national independence, and so on? There are several important distinctions in modern terrorist activity: the differences between domestic and international terrorism and the role of states or governments in promoting terrorist groups in different parts of the world. Terrorists use many weapons in conducting their campaigns of violence. Despite widespread fears about WMD, most terrorist attacks, even today, involve bombs and guns, not highly sophisticated WMD devices.

NEXT

Many young people, and adults, believe that terrorism began

on September 11, 2001, with the al Qaeda attacks on the World Trade Center and the Pentagon. This is not the case. This type of violence has a long history. If we are to understand the nature of terrorism and where it is likely to appear in the future, it is important for us to understand when and where it has appeared in the past.

To aid in developing this understanding, the next chapters describe the history of terrorist violence from its religious origins in the distant past to its contemporary development around the world. This volume's final chapter offers an account of how governments, particularly democratic ones, have sought to overcome the serious challenges posed by this type of violence.

When did terrorism begin? Is it a new development, something that appeared on the world stage very recently? According to many young people, the answer to the latter question is "yes." Terrorism began with a series of attacks staged by al Qaeda, or the followers of Osama bin Laden, against American targets in the United States and abroad, the most notorious of which were the 9/11 massacres at the World Trade Center and the Pentagon. Television news shows that suicide car bombings have become an almost daily occurrence on the streets of Baghdad and other Iraqi cities since the collapse of Saddam Hussein's dictatorship in spring 2003. The fact that terrorism is headline news does not mean that this type of violence began yesterday or the day before, however. Terrorism's presence is by no means new: In one form or another, it has been around for a long time. This chapter recounts the story of terrorism from its origins to the present time.

EARLY HISTORY

The roots of terrorism are ancient. They are to be found in a certain tradition of Greek civilization and, perhaps more important, in the violence of several religiously inspired groups in Jewish, Muslim, Christian, and Hindu traditions.

The Greeks

In the case of the Greeks, the tradition is that of tyrannicide. The philosopher Aristotle (384–322 B.C.) and his successors understood tyranny to be the worst form of government. A tyrant is a ruler who seizes and then holds power illegally, usually on the basis of physical force. Such an individual has little concern for the public good or the interests of the community as a whole. The tyrant rules in his own interests or in the interests of his immediate family and coterie of friends (a modern example would be Saddam Hussein), becoming rich and powerful at the expense of the public. The rule of a tyrant is characterized by its extreme cruelty. Tyrants torture and kill suspected opponents (real or imagined) because it gives them pleasure and because they are intensely suspicious. Because tyrants develop an insatiable need to be flattered, after a while they tend to lose all sense of reality. They are almost literally out of control. Under these circumstances, what can be done to bring an end to tyranny and restore orderly or lawful government?

According to Aristotle, tyranny invites conspiracies aimed at bringing it to an end. The conspiracy might be a small group of plotters, such as the Roman senators who killed the Roman dictator Julius Caesar in 44 B.C. or Emperor Caligula in the following century. Single individuals also often seek to end tyranny by killing the tyrant.

In Book V of his *Politics,* Aristotle states, "There are two chief motives which induce men to attack tyrannies: hatred and contempt. Hatred of tyrants is inevitable, and contempt is also a frequent cause of their destruction."[4] Tyrants' cruelty gives rise to hatred, and their lives of luxury (think of Saddam Hussein's many palaces) give rise to contempt, especially among subjects who struggle to survive in poverty.

The assassination of tyrants for political motives is an ancient practice. It certainly bears some resemblance to modern terrorism. It is not the same, however, because the primary purpose of tyrannicide is simply to get rid of the tyrant, not to send a message to a wider audience of observers. Small groups whose members were killed on behalf of some religious principles, however, closely resemble modern terrorist groups, who act in order to send a message.

The Zealots

Among the oldest of such groups found in the historical record are the Sicarii, a small sect of Zealots, who were active in the Jewish struggle to end Roman rule in Palestine (A.D. 66–73) and whose activities were chronicled by the Roman historian Josephus. According to Josephus (A.D. 37–100), the Zealot movement was founded by Judah the Galilean, an early rabbi who organized a brief uprising against Roman direct rule and taxation.

Roman Senator and Philosopher Cicero on Tyrants

There can be no such thing as fellowship with tyrants, nothing but bitter feud is possible. And it is not repugnant to nature to despoil, if you can, those whom it is a virtue to kill; nay, this pestilent and godless brood should be utterly banished from human society. For, as we amputate a limb in which the blood and the vital spirit has ceased to circulate . . . so monsters, who, under human guise, conceal the cruelty and ferocity of a wild beast, should be severed from the common body of humanity.*

---

* Cicero, "No Fellowship with Tyrants," in Walter Laqueur (ed.), *Voices of Terror*. New York: Reed Press, 2004, p. 18.

The Zealots believed that they were living in the End Times, a period immediately preceding the divine intervention that would put an end to human history. Before the latter could happen, the Zealots believed, the world needed to be purified and purged of its corruptions. Judah the Galilean had taught that Jews could be ruled only by God, not by secular governments like that of Rome. In practical terms, this meant bringing an end to Roman rule in Jerusalem, site of the Holy Temple, and in Judea more generally. How could this be accomplished? The Romans were the foremost military power in the world and rulers of a vast empire.

The Sicarii (the name is taken from the type of daggers they employed) pursued a strategy aimed at provoking the Romans to carry out acts of indiscriminate violence against the Jews. In turn, the Sicarii hoped, the Jews would respond by taking up arms against the Romans to drive them from this province of their empire. The likelihood that this project could succeed must have seemed remote. The power of Rome would have appeared overwhelming. The Sicarii knew better, or at least thought that they knew better. God would intervene in human affairs on behalf of the Jewish rebels and thereby make up for their numerical and military inferiority.[5]

The Sicarii proceeded as follows. At feast days and at other times when large crowds gathered in Jerusalem, an individual would suddenly emerge from the crowd and stab a moderate Jewish leader (someone who advocated collaboration with the Romans), a local Greek resident of Judea, or a member of the Roman occupying power to death using a short dagger or *sica*. The murderer would then disappear back into the crowd. News of the killing would spread quickly throughout the city. Rabbinical authorities also report that the Sicarii burned granaries and sought to sabotage the Jerusalem water supply. An even greater provocation occurred when a band of Sicarii killed a small detachment of Roman soldiers after they had surrendered and laid down their weapons. The Romans carried out a series of reprisals against members of the Jewish community.

These violent activities provoked the Romans as well as the Jews. The situation became polarized as those who counseled moderation were silenced by either violence or fear. The Sicarii got what they wanted: full-scale war. The results of what Josephus labeled "The Jewish War" (A.D. 66–73) were disastrous, at least from the point of view of the Jews. Jerusalem was sacked and the Second Temple burned to the ground. Many Jews were enslaved by Roman masters. In fact, the Arch of Titus, next to the Coliseum in Rome, contains a bas-relief (or sculpture) that depicts Jewish slaves being driven through Rome after their failed uprising. Remnants of the Zealot group fled Jerusalem and took refuge on top of a tabletop mountain known as Masada on the shores of the Dead Sea, where they held off a Roman legion for a few years. Eventually, as the Romans threatened to overrun the defenders, all or most of the Zealots committed suicide rather than become captives.

What makes the violent campaign waged by the Zealot movement in Roman Palestine during the first century A.D. resemble modern terrorism? The answer is not the killing per se, but the audience(s) for whom it was performed. The Sicarii were clearly sending messages. They were sending a message to Jews who wished for a peaceful adjustment to Roman rule. They were also sending a violent message to the Romans that was aimed at provoking them into an indiscriminate reaction against all Jews, not merely those who had taken up arms against their rule. They also were, or at least hoped they were, sending a message to God in the hope that their actions would prompt divine intervention in their struggle to defeat the Romans and thus the advent of a messianic era.

The Assassins

Similar reasoning was at work with the Assassins. The now commonly used word *assassin* comes from the Arabic word for "hashish eaters," a term that Christian Crusaders heard applied to this sect during the eleventh century A.D. The Assassins were a messianic sect within the larger community of Shi'ite Muslims that believed that the original vision of the prophet Mohammed had been corrupted by the largely Sunni leaders of medieval Islam. In order to restore the vision and prepare the way for the arrival of the Mahdi, the Holy Redeemer, the Muslim community (or *umma*) needed to be purified. The founder of the Assassins, Hassan Sibai, or the "Old Man from the Mountain," recognized that his followers were few but his enemies were many, and they could employ powerful military forces. A direct attack would not succeed. Instead, he and his successors adopted the use of *fedayeen*, people who were prepared to sacrifice themselves. Operating in Persia (now Iran) and Syria, young fedayeen were first taught what awaited them on entry into Paradise. The young men prepared to sacrifice themselves were shown an earthly version of Paradise at the Assassins' mountain hideaway. This environment was an oasis of pleasant streams, green foliage, abundant food, and pretty girls.

After this, fedayeen were sent on their missions. Operating in disguise, they sought employment in the households of powerful Sunni leaders. Until the Assassins were destroyed by the Mongol conquerors of the Middle East in the thirteenth century, they managed to murder a long list of prefects, governors, and caliphs. The Assassins regarded these killings as sacramental acts. Over time, they made their way into the inner circles of their victims, and at a time when the targets were least suspicious, the fedayeen would take out daggers (no other type of weapon was used) and stab the victims to death. At that point, the killer would not run away; instead he remained next to the body of his victim and awaited his execution at the hands of the victim's followers. Their willingness to be killed in this way led some observers to the conclusion that the fedayeen must be high on hashish, hence the term "hashish eaters," or Assassins. The killers were not intoxicated; instead, they saw ʾselves as performing religious deeds.

European Christians

Religiously motivated violence of the kind associated with the Zealots and the Assassins is not unknown in the Christian tradition either. During what historian Norman Cohn has referred to as the "pursuit of the millennium,"[6] the period of the Crusades in the centuries after the year 1000, small bands, typically led by self-proclaimed "prophets," appeared in various parts of Europe. These "prophets" proclaimed the beginning of the millennium, a struggle between good and evil leading to the Second Coming and the end of human history. For these Last Times to start, a number of things had to occur. First, Jerusalem, with its Christian holy sites, had to be seized from the hands of the unbelievers, its Muslim rulers. Second, Europe, or "Christendom," as it was known, had to be purified. In practical terms, this meant assaults by Crusade-bound bands—such as the Children's Crusade, the cult of the "Free Spirits," and the Taborites—on wealthy landowners and local Catholic bishops, both seen as corrupt. Above all, though, it meant attacks on Jews. Jews were labeled "Christ killers" whose presence in Christendom posed a threat to those who regarded the millennium as imminent. Oftentimes, Jews, particularly those from communities located around the Danube and Rhine rivers, were confronted by a choice of either forceful conversion to Christianity or death. Many chose death.

Later in European history, during the Protestant Reformation of the sixteenth and seventeenth centuries, there was a renewal of belief in the advent of the millennium. In cities such as Münster, Germany, armed millennial groups like the Anabaptists killed both Catholics and followers of Luther in the belief that they were purging a corrupt world and hastening the End.

Hindus

Killing in order to achieve a religious purpose was not limited to the world's three major monotheistic religions. In India, a

Hindu sect known as the Thugs believed that they had to sacrifice another Hindu in order to satisfy Kali, the goddess of death. To perform this act of ritual sacrifice, members of the sect would befriend someone traveling through their region of India. At a time when the man's trust had been won, a Thug would take out a piece of rope and strangle the person to death. The British put an end to this practice when they colonized India. Other places in Asia abounded with secret societies whose members killed strangers for a variety of secular and religious purposes.

What sets the Zealots, the Assassins, and the Christian millennial groups apart from the others is the mix of religious and political purposes behind the violence. In these three cases, the groups involved were extremist bands on the fringes of the world's major monotheistic religions who sought to send messages to both divine and earthly audiences in the hope of accelerating the end of human history. In order to achieve this goal, the world needed to be cleansed of corrupt and wicked elements. The cleansing almost always involved the use of violence against these elements, at times and places where victims were least likely to expect it and where the perpetrators could expect to achieve maximum publicity.

THE FRENCH REVOLUTION AND AFTER
The Jacobins

The term *terrorism* entered the English language at the time of the French Revolution, the world-shaking event that brought down the French monarchy at the end of the eighteenth century. The "Reign of Terror," or *regime de la terreur*, refers to a time (1793–1794) during the revolution when the Jacobins, a radical group headed by a lawyer named Maximilien Robespierre, took control of the French government. Robespierre and the Jacobins announced that they had uncovered lists of traitors, mostly foreigners, who intended to betray the revolution to its enemies. These traitors needed to be eliminated for the revolution to succeed and for a new world based on "liberty, equality, and fraternity" to be achieved. Accordingly, the Jacobins used their control of the Committee of General Security and the Revolutionary Tribunal to arrest and execute thousands of these perceived subversives. In summer 1794, the Jacobins were toppled from power because of their excesses and Robespierre was sent to the guillotine.

What relationship does the French Reign of Terror have to modern terrorism? At first view, the answer would have to be "not much." This campaign of terrorism was carried out not by a private insurgent group or organization but by those in control of the government. In that regard, the Reign of Terror bears a closer resemblance to the activities of twentieth-century dictatorships like those of Nazi Germany or Stalinist Russia than to Osama bin Laden's al Qaeda or the other organizations described later in this volume. There is, however, a certain resemblance that should be considered.

First, the perpetrators of the terrorist campaign, the Jacobins, were members of a small extremist sect in a wider movement. They saw themselves as carrying out a mission that was, if not divine, then certainly based on a higher cause. Instead of claiming religious inspiration, the Jacobins asserted that their actions were justified in the name of the people. The people, properly understood, could do no wrong. Anything and everything that could be done to advance the cause of the people was perfectly justified. It is not hard to find echoes of the Zealots and the Assassins in the Jacobins' message. For the Jacobins, as for the Zealots and Assassins, the people had replaced God, and the Jacobins believed that only they had the correct understanding of the people's will. Modern terrorist groups often view the world in just this way. Only they—usually small, self-selected bands—have uncovered the real truth that others are too shortsighted or misguided to comprehend.

Second, consider the enemy. Ordinarily, guilt or innocence in criminal cases is thought to be based on individual conduct and a sense of personal accountability before the law. In other words, someone is held accountable because of something he or she has done, such as stealing someone's property or physically harming another person. For the Jacobins during the Reign of Terror, guilt or innocence was based on belonging to certain suspect groups in the French population. Aristocrats and servants of aristocrats were likely to be identified as subversive elements. They were likely to be considered criminal not because of what they had done but because of who they were or what they were suspected of believing. This is also the logic of modern terrorism. Modern terrorists attack people whom they regard as enemies not because these individuals have done something but because of who they are or what the terrorists think they represent. Restaurant workers and stockbrokers in the World Trade Center towers were attacked not because of something they had done but because they belonged to a category—Americans—that the terrorists regarded as criminal.

Third, Robespierre and the other Jacobins intended the Reign of Terror to have a psychological effect on a wider audience than just the victims sent to the guillotine. They intended to create an atmosphere of widespread fear among those in the French population who might harbor reservations about the revolutionary cause or about the direction in which their country was heading. Attempting to modify the behavior of some audience—getting inside people's heads—is one of the principal purposes of twenty-first century terrorists as well.

In these three ways, the Jacobins provide a set of precedents useful in understanding the behavior of terrorist groups whose campaigns of violence many of us find so alarming these days.

European Revolutions

The French Revolution and the era of empire (1803–1815) that followed it ended with the Congress of Vienna (1815). Monarchies were restored not only in France, but in all the countries of

This painting shows Maximilien Robespierre being arrested. The chaos of the scene reflects the chaos that followed the French Revolution, during which the concept of "terreur" was first demonstrated.

Europe in which kings, queens, princes, dukes, and other hereditary rulers had been toppled by Napoleon's armies. The dreams and, for some, the nightmares brought on by the revolution did not go away, however. All over the continent during the first half of the nineteenth century there were people committed to the cause of revolution, who wished to make a revolution.

At first in Italy and then in Greece, Hungary, and elsewhere in Europe, various secret societies such as the Order of the Carbonari and the League of the Just developed. These societies were committed to keeping the cause of revolution alive. Members of these clandestine organizations discussed the ways and means of revolution, and all over Europe, including tsarist Russia, writers and philosophers also engaged in disputes over how and under what circumstances a new violent revolution was likely to break out.

What did these new nineteenth-century revolutionaries hope to achieve? The famous slogan of the French Revolution was "Liberty, Equality, Fraternity." In a sense, these three words reflect three distinct aims of the revolutionaries in this era.

Some hoped to foment revolution in the name of liberty (this goal was also foremost in the minds of America's Founding Fathers). The objective was to overthrow monarchies and replace the principle of government based on heredity, the so-called "divine right" of kings, with popular sovereignty, individual liberty, and constitutional government—in another word, democracy.

Other revolutionaries had equality as their fundamental cause. In the nineteenth century, many European countries witnessed the rapid development of modern industry. Accompanying this development was the growth of large classes of manual workers who often earned low wages, worked long hours, and lived impoverished lives with their families in the slums of London, Paris, Milan, Frankfurt, and other major cities. Those who have read the novels of English writer Charles Dickens or seen the films adapted from them will be familiar with these brutal conditions. One of the major effects of these conditions was the emergence of groups of activists and writers who became committed to the cause of socialism. For them, the basic problem was capitalism, the private ownership of industrial enterprises and the vast inequalities it created between rich and poor, worker and owner, and middle and working class. For these socialists, the goal of revolution was the overthrow of the capitalist system and its replacement with some system of worker or public ownership of enterprises. The aim was the establishment of economic and social equality— not "equality of opportunity," in which Americans usually believe, but a kind of equality of condition.

The third ideal, fraternity, also became an important cause of revolutionary activity during the nineteenth century. "Fraternity," or the goal of national independence, excited the

imagination of revolutionaries who wanted to free their nations
or peoples from the control of the various European empires.
Many ethnic groups or "nations" of the nineteenth century were
not organized as separate states but formed part of the British,
French, Austro-Hungarian, Russian, and Ottoman empires.
Ireland was part of the British Empire, much of Poland was
part of the Russian Empire, and the Balkans were divided
between the Austro-Hungarian and Ottoman empires. The aim
of many nationalist revolutionaries was to free their respective
homelands from the empires, a goal that has come to be called
"national liberation."

Nineteenth-century Revolutionaries

Support for revolution on behalf of liberty, equality, or fraternity
is not equivalent to support for or the use of terrorism.
Nonetheless, it was in the context of these nineteenth-century
debates and discussions among would-be revolutionaries that
modern ideas about terrorism emerged. German radical demo-
crat Karl Heinzen (1809–1880) is widely regarded as the first
modern writer to suggest a rationale for the use of terrorism.
In his 1849 essay "Murder," Heinzen argued that murder has
been the principal agent of human progress. He agreed that the
voluntary killing of another human being is a crime but
noted that governments authorize such killings all the time. If
governments can kill, why cannot those opposed to them, particularly when the governments that carry out killings have not
been chosen by those they seek to rule? Heinzen wrote, "It seems
that moral reactions to murder are closely linked to the self-
interest of those reacting. . . ."[7] In making his case, Heinzen
produced arguments widely used by advocates of terrorism in
our own time: The government or "the other side" started it first,
they are only using tactics already employed by those in power,
and the justice or injustice of killing depends on the point of
view of the observer. If the observer supports the government,
he or she will support its voluntary taking of human life; if the

observer supports the revolutionary cause, he or she will oppose government killing but will support killing if it advances the goal of revolution.

Heinzen went on to express some strikingly modern thoughts about revolutionary tactics:

> The greatest benefactor of mankind will be he who makes it possible for a few men to wipe out thousands. So when we hear that train-loads of murderers' accomplices have been hurled from the track by a thimble of fulminating silver placed under the rails; or that bombs . . . have been placed beneath paving stones in order to tear apart whole companies of invading barbarians . . . ; or that, perhaps, containers filled with poison, which burst in the air, can rain down ruin on entire regiments . . . then in such methods we shall perceive only to what desperate measures the party of freedom has been driven by the . . . party of the barbarians.[8]

The tactics that Heinzen advocated involve the use of highly lethal explosives and poisons by small bands of highly motivated revolutionaries to cause mayhem ("wipe out thousands") among the accomplices—the police and the military—of despotic governments, as Heinzen defines despotism. These ideas, which come to us from the middle of the nineteenth century, are very close to the tactics adopted by terrorists and their defenders in the first decade of the twenty-first century.

Another revolutionary, Sergey Nechaev (1847–1882), who wrote a decade after Heinzen, produced a pamphlet entitled "Catechism of the Revolutionist" (1869) that provided some basic rules for the conduct of a terrorist campaign in the cause (in this case socialist) of revolution. Nechaev's remarks represent a guide for revolutionaries—how they should behave in order to best promote their objectives. In this regard, he stressed that those committed to the cause should think of themselves as thoroughly separated from the rest of society and should feel completely indifferent to its culture and values. Revolutionaries, Nechaev continued, need to become cold-blooded killers who come to recognize that they are likely "doomed" to be killed by the police. To be effective, true revolutionaries need to organize themselves into small, clandestine bands ready to strike out at the government and representatives of the old order as opportunities to do so arise. In fact, Nechaev drew up a list of categories of people to be killed. He wrote:

> In compiling these lists and deciding the order referred to above, the guiding principle must not be individual acts of villainy committed by the person, nor even by the hatred he provokes among the society or its people. This villainy and hatred, however, may to a certain extent be useful, since they help to incite popular rebellion. The guiding principle must be the measure of service the person's death will necessarily render to the revolutionary cause. Therefore, in the first instance all those must be annihilated who are especially harmful to the revolutionary organization, and whose sudden and violent deaths will also inspire the greatest fear in the government and, by depriving it of its cleverest and most energetic figures, will shatter its strength.[9]

Heinzen's and Nechaev's remarks were not made in a vacuum. In 1848, there were popular uprisings all over Europe; almost all failed to produce the desired changes. In France, mobs in Paris succeeded in sending the king, Louis Philippe, into exile and establishing a short-lived democracy. This democracy was replaced by the dictatorship of Louis-Napoleon (the emperor's nephew) within a few years. These were also the years in which the young Karl Marx and Friedrich Engels wrote the *Communist Manifesto*, an appeal for working-class revolution against the capitalist system. This revolution was not based on utopian ideas but on scientific—or allegedly scientific—principles concerning the failures and contradictions inherent in the private ownership of industry.

The 1850s and 1860s also constitute a period in which individuals attempted to murder leading political figures. In January 1858, an Italian nationalist named Felice Orsini attempted to assassinate Louis-Napoleon by throwing a bomb at his carriage as it arrived in front of the Paris Opera House. The ruler was unharmed, but the explosion killed eight passersby. Orsini sought to kill Louis-Napoleon because he had stationed troops in Rome to protect the Vatican against efforts to create a unified Italian state, efforts opposed by the Catholic Church, and to make the Eternal City its capital.

Orsini inspired others. On July 14, 1861, a young German law student from Leipzig attempted to assassinate the king of Prussia because of his failure to unify Germany. Five years later, Otto von Bismarck, the Prussian chancellor, was the target of an assassination attempt by another university student. In 1878, after the achievement of German unity, Emperor Wilhelm was the victim of two attempted assassinations, on these occasions by individuals acting on behalf of worker revolution. These failed assassinations of some of Europe's crowned heads were politically motivated to be sure, but they do not quite fit this book's definition of terrorism (see chapter 1) as a type of violence carried out by insurgent groups and intended to send a message to an audience. The first modern groups that do fit this definition, ones that waged campaigns of "propaganda by deed," are the subject of the next chapter.

CHAPTER 3

MODERN TERRORISM:
THE FIRST WAVE

Modern terrorism, political violence that would be recognizable as terrorism to people today, is a product of the last few decades of the nineteenth century and the first decade and a half of the twentieth, the years that led up to the outbreak of World War I (1914–1918) in particular. In this period, mass circulation newspapers and magazines throughout Europe and North America carried lurid stories about a secret worldwide conspiracy of terrorists aimed at destroying governments and bringing down all established authority.

The result was widespread public fear about the terrorist threat caused by the occasional bomb set off in a public space or the widely publicized assassination of a renowned political figure. The explosion in May 1886 at Haymarket Square in Chicago during a workers' protest that killed several policemen, and the murder of Italy's King Umberto in Monza in the summer of 1900 are examples. Countries throughout the Western world enacted new laws aimed at putting an end to the wave of violence. Important writers, such as Joseph Conrad (*The Secret Agent*) and Fyodor Dostoevsky (*The Possessed*), wrote novels and other works of fiction about the murky world of terrorist violence. Terrorism experts emerged and had their say. Italian criminologist Cesare Lombroso saw a connection between bomb-throwing and certain vitamin deficiencies and various physical ailments. Then, as in our own time, terrorism had defenders who defined its perpetrators as heroic self-sacrificers, martyrs willing to lay down their lives on behalf of oppressed people. For these defenders, the victims of terrorist violence deserved what they got because of their previous acts of wrongdoing. Consequently, those killed by terrorism were really its perpetrators. Properly understood, the killers really aimed at liberating mankind from suffering.

The role of science also came under discussion. The advocates and defenders of terrorism at the end of the nineteenth century, such as German-American revolutionary Johann Most (1846–1906), viewed the discovery of dynamite with great approval because of its potential for advancing the cause. (Most worked at a dynamite factory in New Jersey.) Small groups could now easily kill large numbers of enemies. For the terrorists, dynamite could serve as a "force multiplier," making them more powerful than their numbers would suggest. It might even be possible, Most reasoned, to conduct a revolution on a more scientific basis. Instead of large mobs of revolutionaries taking to the streets of Paris or Berlin and confronting the well-armed forces of the government, advances in weaponry like dynamite would make it possible for the revolution to succeed with a minimum loss of life. Most conceived of a scenario in which a handful of revolutionaries might bring down the government by dropping a bomb from a low-flying hot-air balloon on a military parade, thereby killing off its entire upper echelon of politicians and military officers with only a minimum loss of life to ordinary soldiers and civilians.

For those who have paid attention to terrorist violence not at the end of the nineteenth century but in the first years of the twenty-first, all of this will sound familiar. There are some dramatic differences—religious fanatics did not play a major role in the first wave of modern terrorism—but the number of similarities seems sufficient to leave the impression that, in the twenty-first century, we are dealing with the same kind of activity: political terrorism.

NINETEENTH-CENTURY TERRORISM

Russia

Liberty, as opposed to equality or fraternity, has rarely been a fundamental motive in the launching of a terrorist campaign. In the case of the tsarist autocracy in Russia in the last few decades of the nineteenth century, though, the pursuit of liberty mixed with the long-term goal of equality is key to understanding the first modern terrorist organization, the Narodnaia Volia, or People's Will (1879–1894). Narodnaia Volia was an organization that consisted largely of young people, many of them university students, who had hoped to "go to the people" and win their support for a revolutionary uprising against the authoritarian rule of the Russian tsars, at that time Alexander II. Their goal was to replace tsarist rule with a new constitutional and democratic system that would, in turn, make Russia's transformation into a socialist society possible. Their attempts to mobilize the country's vast peasant population met with little success. "The people" and the young, largely urban and middle-class students couldn't understand each other. By and large, the Russian peasantry, recently freed from serfdom, was interested in eking out a living, whereas the students expressed themselves in terms of abstract and lofty ideals.

In the wake of this failed effort to win the masses over to the revolutionary cause during the early and mid-1870s, the

Perhaps not the most terrible of the Russian tsars, Alexander II was nonetheless hated by his people. The first modern terrorist group, Narodnaia Volia, was formed during Alexander's reign to oppose tsarist rule.

People's Will turned to urban terrorism. At first, the violence took the form of retaliation against tsarist officials who had tortured or killed members of People's Will who had been taken into police custody. In 1878, a young woman named Vera

Zasulich shot the governor-general of St. Petersburg because he had ordered the flogging of a prisoner for not removing his hat during an inspection of the prison yard. Zasulich's gesture and others like them seemed to win popular sympathy for the organization. As a consequence, members of the People's Will sought to take advantage of the tactic. In 1880, its executive committee drew up a program that called for the assassination of the most harmful leaders of the tsarist regime as well as individuals identified as police spies and traitors to the organization. Serious acts of government brutality against the people in general would be met with more assassinations. This campaign of terror was intended to have a psychological effect: It was a tool to show ordinary Russians that the government was vulnerable and that they did not have to suffer endlessly at the hands of the tsar's officials. The violence would be used to sow terror among the latter and raise the morale of those who witnessed their confusion.

The Russian People's Will, The First Modern Terrorist Group

For the Narodnya Volya [People's Will], the apathy and alienation of the Russian masses afforded few alternatives to the resort to daring and dramatic acts of violence designed to attract attention to the group and its cause. However, unlike the many late twentieth century terrorist organizations who have cited the principle of "propaganda by deed" to justify the wanton targeting of civilians in order to assure them publicity through the shock and horror produced by wholesale bloodshed, the Narodnya Volya displayed an almost quixotic attitude to the violence they wrought. To them, "propaganda by deed" meant the selective targeting of specific individuals whom the group considered of the autocratic, oppressive state.*

* Bruce Hoffman. *Inside Terrorism*. New York: Columbia University Press, 1999, p. 18.

Based on these ideas, members of the People's Will carried out a series of assassinations over the next few years. The most spectacular of these murders was the assassination of Tsar Alexander II in St. Petersburg in 1881. This act led to a massive police crackdown on the People's Will and the arrest of virtually all of its leaders. There was no revolution, at least in the immediate aftermath of the crackdown, but the People's Will's "achievement" brought a new wave of youthful recruits to the organization, along with a number of copycat groups that employed terrorism on and off for more than a decade after the killing of Alexander II.

Another significant and sustained terrorist campaign in Russia was launched at the beginning of the twentieth century, this time by a group known as the Socialist Revolutionaries, or SR. The SR was a Marxist organization committed to bringing Marx's brand of socialism to what many regarded as a socially backward society. The SR became a rival of another Marxist group, the Russian Social Democratic Party, from which V.I. Lenin and the Bolsheviks emerged.

In 1901–1902, the SR took advantage of the government's violent repression of university protests to recruit a large number of students to the revolutionary cause and to the Combat Organization, the branch of the party organized to carry out terrorist attacks on the most visible symbols of the tsarist autocracy. The principal targets of the Combat Organization were local governors, state ministers, factory managers, and police officials, who often had earned reputations for their cruelty and whose elimination, the SR hoped, would win widespread popular approval. Among the most spectacular of the killings was that of the Russian minister of the interior, A.P. Sipiagian, in 1902 and, later, the assassination of Grand Duke Serge Alexandrovich. The SR was clearly committed to the revolutionary goal of equality. The party did have certain scruples about the use of terrorism, however: The SR leadership did not support the use of terrorist violence against constitutional regimes such as those that existed in France, Great Britain, and the United States. When Tsar Nicholas II issued a manifesto in 1905 that called for the formation of a Russian parliament, or duma, the SR Combat Organization suspended its operations until it became clear that this new institution would not set Russia on the path to constitutional democracy.

The SR did not lead the 1917 revolution that brought down the tsar and replaced the monarchy with a Communist dictatorship over the next few years. Lenin and his Bolshevik followers led the way. In fact, after a brief period of tolerance, the Bolshevik police ruthlessly repressed the SR and the remnants of its Combat Organization.

Socialism and Anarchy

Both Lenin's Communists (or Bolsheviks) and the Russian Socialist Revolutionaries were Marxists. They were committed to the ideas of Karl Marx (1818–1883), the mid-nineteenth-century German revolutionary writer and activist whose works on the "inevitability" of working-class revolution against an allegedly doomed capitalist system inspired thousands of revolutionaries throughout the world.

Marx's role as the leader and foremost theorist of the cause of socialist revolution did not go unchallenged: The efforts of his rival, Mikhail Bakunin (1814–1876), and his successors must be considered. Bakunin and a long list of European and American revolutionaries, including Peter Kropotkin, Errico Malatesta, Carlo Pisacane, Emma Goldman, and Johann Most, were anarchists who believed that the twin evils of private property and government would have to be eliminated for humans to be truly free and equal. To quote American historian Barbara Tuchman:

> The Anarchists believed that with Property, the Monarch of all evils, eliminated, no man could again live off the labor of another and human nature would be released to seek its natural level of justice among men. The role of

the State would be replaced by voluntary cooperation among individuals and the role of law by the supreme law of the general welfare. To this end no reform of existing social evils through vote or persuasion was of any use, for the ruling class would never give up its property or the powers and laws which protected ownership of property. Therefore, the necessity of violence [sic]. Only revolutionary overturn of the entire malignant system would accomplish the desired result.[10]

How was this "revolutionary overturn" to be achieved? Most anarchists did not believe it would occur spontaneously when the social and political conditions became intolerable for most of the oppressed. Nor, for that matter, were they persuaded that careful planning and organization were required to prepare the way. When Lenin and his followers referred to the so-called "vanguard of the proletariat," they had in mind the crucial role to be played by a political party of full-time militants whose job was to raise the level of revolutionary awareness among the masses. Because they seemed to lead to hierarchy and leadership groups, the anarchists were skeptical of organizations in general, even ones that claimed to foment revolution. What these nineteenth- and early twentieth-century revolutionaries came to stand for was "propaganda by deed."

Single individuals or small decentralized bands could spark a revolution, the anarchists believed, by committing spectacular acts of violence against hated symbols of the state and the capitalist system, "captains of industry" in particular. These deeds would prove infinitely more important than street-corner speeches and revolutionary proclamations in showing the masses just how vulnerable the existing system was. Acts of armed propaganda (or propaganda by deed) would then set off a general conflagration.

The 1890s and the first years of the new century witnessed a wave of anarchist assassinations and bombings. The United

States was not immune. In 1892, Alexander Berkman almost succeeded in killing Henry Clay Frick, the vice president of the Carnegie Steel Company, and in 1901, another anarchist, Leon Czolgosz, assassinated U.S. president William McKinley. A year earlier, an Italian immigrant to the United States, Gaetano Bresci (a member of an anarchist "circle" in Paterson, New Jersey), returned to his native country and shot King Umberto to death. In 1894, French president Marie François Sadi Carnot was stabbed to death by a young anarchist angered by his refusal to pardon another anarchist convicted of violent activities. In Spain during these years, Premier Antonio Cánovas became the victim of an anarchist assassination, as did his counterpart in Argentina. Perhaps the most spectacular of these murders during what came to be called the "Era of the Attempts" (i.e., the period around the turn of the twentieth century when anarchists attempted to assassinate heads of state and other political figures throughout Europe) was the assassination of Empress Elizabeth of Austria-Hungary in 1898. She was stabbed to death by an Italian immigrant in Switzerland.

The anarchists did not limit themselves to the gun and the dagger. They also threw bombs. In Barcelona in 1896, a bomb was thrown at a religious procession. The targets were the local bishop and the city's military governor. They escaped unhurt, but the explosion killed 11 people and left more than 40 wounded. Later, in 1906, other Spanish anarchists hurled a bomb at King Alfonso and his bride after their wedding ceremony. The explosion left the monarch unharmed but killed 20 passersby. In France, one anarchist threw a bomb onto the floor of the Chamber of Deputies, and others set off explosions in the crowded Café Terminus and the fashionable Restaurant Foyot on the grounds that their customers were "bourgeois" and consequently guilty beneficiaries of the existing system of oppression.

Nowhere in the Western world did these and similar acts of terrorism succeed in sparking the revolution for which the anarchists had hoped. If anything, they tended to scare the public and, as a result, set back the cause of the movement. Most of the governments in the countries affected by this spectacular surge of political violence, including the United States, enacted new laws aimed at making it easier for the police to detain anarchists suspected of planning violence or, in some instances, people suspected of sympathizing with their goals.

Nationalist Movements

Fraternity, or nationalism, also provided a cause of terrorist violence in this era. It was a time in which much of the world was controlled by one or another of the European empires: British, French, Austro-Hungarian, Russian, and Ottoman. These empires were typically multinational in the sense that they contained various "nations" or "peoples" often with distinct histories, languages, customs, and religious practices. For these nations, the goal of revolution was not the end of capitalism or monarchical absolutism but the achievement of national independence. This cause continues to provide an important basis for terrorist violence even in our own time.

The cause of Irish independence from Britain was the first nationalist revolutionary movement from which terrorism appeared in the last decades of the nineteenth century. Earlier in the century, an organization known as the Irish Republican Brotherhood (IRB) had attempted an open insurrection against British rule, but the efforts failed completely. In the wake of the IRB defeat, three groups that were prepared to use clandestine violence in order to get the British out of Ireland emerged. In the 1880s, a group of Irish-Americans known in Gaelic as the Clan na Gael employed the newly discovered substance dynamite to set off explosions in British-owned buildings. No one was killed. The Irish National Invincibles, an organization headed by Jeremiah O'Donovan Rossa, was responsible for the Phoenix Park murders—the assassination of Lord Frederick Cavendish, Britain's newly appointed chief secretary for Ireland,

and his assistant in Dublin on May 6, 1882—and several other attempted terrorist acts over the course of the decade.

The Irish were hardly alone in making use of the bomb and the gun. In the 1890s, the Armenian Revolutionary Federation (ARF), inspired to some extent by the example of the Russian People's Will organization, carried out terrorist attacks against both Russian and Ottoman officials as part of its effort to create an independent country of Armenia. Likewise and at about the same time, a group that called itself the Internal Macedonian Revolutionary Organization (IMRO) appeared. Its goal was to create an independent state out of the part of the Ottoman Empire that today forms parts of Greece, Bulgaria, and Serbia. As in the case of the ARF, IMRO's terrorist campaign against Turkish officials came to nothing. In this case, the terrorism also did not lead to a tragic and massive wave of killings carried out against civilians by the Turkish military as happened to the Armenians during World War I.

Terrorism in the Balkans led to events that provided the immediate spark for the outbreak of World War I in 1914. In 1908, Austria-Hungary took control of the province of Bosnia-Herzegovina. Various Serbian nationalist groups expressed their outrage because they had hoped to make this former Ottoman territory a part of a greater Serbia. The Narodna Obrana (People's Defense) and other pan-Serb groups staged terrorist attacks against targets in Bosnia. A competing organization, Young Bosnia, whose goal was the establishment of a unified state for all southern Slavic peoples—Slovenians, Croats, Bosnians, and Serbs—was formed. It was prepared to use violence against the Hapsburg Empire toward this end. A very young Bosnian student by the name of Gavrilo Princip was responsible for the assassination of Archduke Franz Ferdinand, the heir to the crown of Austria-Hungary, in Sarajevo on June 28, 1914. (Princip, along with several other members of Young Bosnia, had formed a clandestine band known as the Black Hand.) This attack set the events in motion that led to the outbreak of World War I in August 1914.

BACKLASH TERRORISM

The terrorist activities discussed to this point are those whose perpetrators hoped their violence would unleash revolutionary changes of one kind or another. Terrorism is a tactic, however, not an ideology. It may be used by groups with a variety of goals and objectives; the groups who employ them do not need to have a complex set of ideas to explain their actions. In fact, terrorist violence may be used by organizations that hope to block social and political changes they oppose. Often, these groups form as a backlash against the possibility of such changes.

The Ku Klux Klan

One obvious example of this kind of backlash terrorism is the Ku Klux Klan. The first Klan—there have been several successor generations—was organized by veterans of the Confederate armed forces after the Civil War (1861–1865). When General Nathan Bedford Forrest and other veterans of the War Between the States organized the Klan in 1867, they aimed to prevent the South's newly freed slaves from exercising the rights they acquired from the Thirteenth, Fourteenth, and Fifteenth Amendments to the U.S. Constitution. During the almost decade-long period of Reconstruction after the war, hooded and robed Klansmen throughout the South waged a campaign of terrorism that involved shootings, burnings, and lynchings intended to deny African Americans the right to vote in elections and to participate in political life more generally. Klan violence was also intended to terrify this newly freed population into accepting a system of racial segregation and subordinate status within this arrangement. There were clearly other forces at work, but the Klan's terrorism continued to play a role in sustaining this system for almost the entire century after the end of the Civil War. In fact, America's first major motion picture, D.W. Griffith's wildly popular *Birth of a Nation* (1915), was a celebration of the Klansmen's so-called "heroic" defense of the white supremacy.

Europe

In Europe in the two decades between the end of World War I in 1918 and the outbreak of World War II in 1939, there was another outbreak of this kind of backlash terrorism. Some

Backlash Terrorism

Most of us are aware that the United States is a principal target of terrorist groups throughout the world. The 9/11 attacks and the fighting under way in Iraq make this point abundantly clear. Fewer of us, however, realize that the United States has had homegrown terrorists for many years.

The Ku Klux Klan carried out terrorist attacks on African Americans during the civil rights struggles of the 1950s and 1960s. The cause of Puerto Rican independence led to a wave of terrorist bombings in New York, Chicago, and Washington, D.C., during the 1970s. On the far left, the Weather Underground and the Symbionese Liberation Army set off bombs, carried out assassinations, and staged bank robberies and kidnappings over the same decade. On the racist and anti-Semitic right, a number of "hate groups," including the Silent Brotherhood, hoped to ignite a racial holy war in the country during the 1980s in the hope that a white supremacist regime would be created. African Americans, Hispanics, and Asian Americans would be deported and the country's Jewish population killed off when the revolution achieved its goals. Timothy McVeigh, a man inspired by these ideas and by fears of a "new world order" conspiracy, detonated a truck-bomb in front of the Alfred P. Murrah Federal Building in Oklahoma City in 1995, an event that killed more people than any other until the 9/11 attacks. In short, even in the absence of militant Islamic groups from the Middle East or South Asia, the United States is not immune to terrorism carried out by a wide range of groups with different political agendas.

background commentary is necessary to understand how and why this occurred.

The Bolshevik Revolution of October 1917 ("Red October") in Russia not only had profound effects on that troubled country, but it also unleashed expectations, throughout much of Europe and beyond, that Communists inspired by the Bolsheviks' success and the ideologies of Marx and Lenin might succeed in sparking social revolutions elsewhere. The conditions in Europe in the years immediately after World War I provided an embittered atmosphere, a background against which these expectations were pursued by social revolutionary bands.

In Budapest, in the newly independent country of Hungary, there was an attempt at Communist revolution under the leadership of a follower of Lenin named Bela Kun. In the immediate aftermath of the war in Germany and against a background of economic and political chaos, revolutionaries seized power briefly in Munich and other parts of Bavaria and proclaimed a Communist republic. In Berlin, the Spartacus group attempted to do the same. In Italy, a revolutionary left emerged from the war and urged factory workers in Turin and Milan to stage sit-in strikes and encouraged peasants and farm laborers to seize large farms owned by wealthy and often absentee landowners in the agricultural lands of the Po River valley. Oftentimes red flags were raised after these land "expropriations."

These developments and the fears that they aroused throughout much of Europe caused a backlash. In Italy, a fascist movement emerged under the leadership of a former socialist by the name of Benito Mussolini (1883–1945). The Fascists, particularly active in the sections of the country where the current of Red revolution was running the strongest, were organized into paramilitary squads of Black Shirts. In 1920–1921, the Black Shirts engaged in what were called "punitive expeditions." These night-time raids included acts of terrorist violence. Leaders of labor unions and peasant-farmer leagues were frequently beaten and sometimes killed as a means of sending a message to all those pushing in the direction of a Red or revolutionary Italy.

In Germany, as in Italy, the forces prepared to use terrorism as a means of ending the social revolutionary threat largely succeeded. At first, the Freikorps, or "Free Corps," composed of discharged World War I veterans, murdered the leaders of what proved to be short-lived Soviet-style Red republics in Bavaria and Berlin. Later, in the 1920s, the Nazi movement under Adolf Hitler engaged in similar practices.

In other parts of Europe, Finland, Romania, Hungary, and Yugoslavia especially, movements whose leaders expressed their admiration for and sought to mimic the Italian Fascist and German Nazi movements emerged. In Romania, the paramilitary Iron Guard murdered a number of leading national politicians, including two former prime ministers whom they believed were taking the country in a leftward direction. In Finland at the end of the 1920s, the Lapua movement (named after the town in which it was formed) was organized for the purpose of bringing an end to Communist influence in that country. Accordingly, during the 1930s, Lapua youth smashed the printing presses of Communist publications and beat and sometimes killed Communist members of parliament and other Reds. In Hungary, a "white terror," led by right-wing military officers, brought an end to Bela Kun's Bolshevik-like republic in Budapest. Yugoslavia's pro-Italian Fascist Ustasha organization succeeded in assassinating King Alexander, along with the French foreign minister, while the king was on a state visit to Marseilles, France, in 1934. In this case, the cause was not blocking advances of the revolutionary left but the pursuit of Croatian independence from Belgrade.

Terrorism driven by a backlash against changes or potential changes in society recurred throughout the twentieth century. In most cases, backlash terrorism does not begin with attacks directed against the national government. Rather, the violence characteristically begins with attacks aimed at groups in the population who are identified with changes in the social and political status quo. In interwar Europe (1919–1939), this usually meant terrorist attacks directed against the revolutionary left—Communists, for example—and those thought to be sympathetic to the left's cause. In other instances, the initial campaign of violence is directed at members of minority ethnic groups who seek to achieve something approaching equality of status with the majority population. The terrorist violence directed against African Americans by white supremacist groups during the civil rights era of the 1950s and 1960s illustrates this point. Oftentimes, when groups engaged in backlash terrorism reach the conclusion that the government is siding with those who seek to change the status quo instead of defending it, they will change targets. Government institutions and government officials are identified as enemies and consequently become appropriate targets for violence.

World War II (1939–1945) was no doubt the most horren-dous armed conflict in human history. Cities were devastated, economies destroyed, and millions of people, many of them civilians, were killed as a result of the fighting. State terrorism is another matter, but political terrorism, the work of relatively small bands of insurgents, did not play a major role in this world-spanning conflict. There was a significant resumption of political terrorism in the years after the war, however. Our attention now focuses there.

ANTICOLONIALISM AND NATIONALISM:
THE SECOND WAVE

The two decades after the end of World War II in 1945 caused political changes of enormous historical significance around the world. Eastern Europe came under the control of the Soviet Union, a result of the Red Army's victory over the Nazi military. A long-term cold war between the Soviets and the United States and its allies over the spread of Communism to other parts of the globe emerged. In China, Communist forces under the leadership of Mao Tse-tung (1893–1976) defeated the Nationalists in 1949 and established the People's Republic of China. Great Britain, France, and other European countries with colonial empires throughout Asia, Africa, and the Middle East were seriously weakened by World War II and began to loosen their grip on their imperial possessions. As a result, there was an end to empire in most places.

In some places, the Europeans left more or less peacefully. The British extended independence to India and Pakistan in 1947. Some years later, in Africa, they did the same with Ghana and Nigeria. In other places, the Europeans chose to fight in order to retain their control. In what is now Indonesia, the Dutch waged a losing battle to maintain their rule over the Dutch East Indies. The French fought an armed Communist insurgency in Indochina, as did the British in Malaya.

The departure of the Europeans and the beginning of national independence did not necessarily mean the onset of a period of peace and tranquility. Sometimes, the new nations' boundaries had been drawn to suit the interests of the colonial power rather than those of the local inhabitants. As a result, in newly independent countries such as Congo, Nigeria, Somalia, and Sri Lanka, members of ethnic groups with little in common or with long-standing animosities found themselves citizens of the same country. Often, the result was a series of internal or civil wars as one group or another struggled for dominance or to secede from the new country. The period between 1945 and the mid-1960s in much of what came to be known as the Third World was characterized by widespread violence.

In most cases, the various "national liberation struggles" and the civil conflicts that sometimes followed them involved guerrilla-style warfare, or what one writer referred to as the "war of the flea."[11] Often following the theories of Mao Tse-tung and other practitioners, insurgents faced with the task of defeating a superior military force established outposts and camps in remote locales, usually hard-to-find places in rain forests and remote mountain ranges. From these hideouts, they usually began their operations by staging armed attacks against thinly protected outposts of government authority. Public buildings, police stations, and sometimes army barracks became the targets of nighttime attacks. Those in the local population identified as collaborators with the colonialists were often attacked as well. At the same time, the insurgents did things aimed at making themselves popular with the area's usually peasant or small-farm population. If this strategy worked, over time, the insurgents wore down the armed forces of the colonial administration to a point that policymakers in London, Paris, Brussels, and the Hague concluded that the benefits of retaining control of the territory were outweighed by the human and material costs of fighting the insurgency. What role existed for terrorism in these developments?

Terrorism played a subordinate role in several national liberation struggles. In Vietnam, for example, the Viet Minh carried out an assassination campaign against French officials and their collaborators in the countryside. On occasion, their cadres in the major cities also hurled bombs in restaurants and other public places where members of the colonial administration were known to congregate. The terrorism in this and other instances was part of the early "agitation-propaganda" phase of the insurgency. Its principal purpose was to mobilize Indochina's farmers and peasants for the long-term guerrilla war to expel the French and create the independent countries of Laos, Cambodia, and Vietnam. Graham Greene's novel *The Quiet American* captured the atmosphere of the end of French rule in this section of Southeast Asia in the early 1950s.

In a handful of places, such as Cyprus, Yemen, and Kenya, terrorism played a central role in bringing an end to colonial domination in this era. The most widely discussed cases are those of Palestine and Algeria.

PALESTINE

The struggle over Palestine in the years immediately after the end of World War II involved three major parties with several concerned and important onlookers. The British had ruled Palestine under a mandate from the League of Nations during the 1920s and 1930s. During this period, a succession of British governments had to contend with two competing nationalisms: Zionist and Palestinian Arab. The Zionist claim for national independence was based on the historical link between the Jewish people and the Land of Israel, from which the Jews had been expelled by the Romans many centuries before the modern era. The modern Zionist movement, which called for a return of the Jewish people to their historic homeland, began in Europe toward the end of the nineteenth century.

In 1917, the British government issued the Balfour Declaration, which indicated its willingness to permit the creation of such a homeland in Palestine. When this area, which had been part of the Ottoman Empire before World War I, fell under British control, Zionist immigrants from Europe and elsewhere began to arrive in pursuit of this homeland. Unfortunately, their arrival became a source of friction for the mandate's Arab inhabitants. On occasion, this friction turned to rioting and violence. The British were caught in the middle. In 1939, as World War II approached, the British government issued a "white paper" (a statement of British government policy based on the recommendations of a Royal Commission) that indicated the imposition of severe restrictions on Jewish immigration. The British enforced this policy throughout the war. When the war ended, leaving approximately 6 million European Jews dead as a result of the Nazis' policy of genocide, the government in London decided to continue its "white paper" policy. In effect, this meant that a few hundred thousand Holocaust survivors who wanted to immigrate would be denied entry into Palestine.

When this happened in 1945, two organizations whose members were drawn from Palestine's Jewish community launched a terrorist campaign designed to get the British out. There was the Irgun, a group led by Menachem Begin, a future Israeli prime minister, and the Stern Gang, or Lehi (*Lohamei Herut Yisrael,* or "Fighters for the Freedom of Israel"). Over the next three years, these groups launched one attack after another. Among the most spectacular was Irgun's bombing of the King

This photo, from December 27, 1947, shows members of the national military organization Irgun Zvai Leumi, a Zionist guerrilla group that began an armed revolt against British rule in Palestine. Irgun was led by Menachem Begin, a future Israeli prime minister.

David Hotel in Jerusalem in 1947, which killed more than 90 people, and Lehi's 1948 assassination of Count Folke Bernadotte, the new United Nations peace negotiator.

In itself, the terrorist violence committed by these small bands of extremists was not sufficient to get the British out. In conjunction with pressure coming from other sources, most notably the United States, the United Nations' fact-finding commission, and the Jewish community in Palestine, however, the British were persuaded to leave the area in 1948 and to permit the establishment of two separate countries on the territory of mandate Palestine. One would be Jewish and called Israel, and the other would be Arab.

Leaders of the Palestinian Arab community and the Arab Higher Committee and Haj Amin al-Husseini, who was the grand mufti of Jerusalem, refused to accept the UN-backed partition plan. They vowed to use violence to prevent the partition of Palestine and the establishment of a Jewish state. In the first months of 1948, as the British were planning their departure, Arab groups launched a series of terrorist attacks against the area's Jewish community. Truck bombings were a favorite method. On one occasion, Arab terrorists stole a British army truck, loaded it with explosives, and then deto-nated it in front of the newspaper offices of the *Jerusalem Post*, killing 15 people. This attack and many others like it were not sufficient to prevent a new Israeli government from declaring the country's independence in May 1948. Of course, having declared independence, the new Israeli state was confronted with an invasion by the armies of the surrounding Arab states, a far more serious challenge than the one posed by the grand mufti's terrorists.

ALGERIA

The uprising against French rule in Algeria, which began in 1953, was the other major case of a national liberation struggle in which terrorism played a significant role. At about the time of the uprising, the French government was willing, with just a little prodding, to grant independence to two other North African countries: Tunisia and Morocco. Algeria was different because of its large population of European settlers. The government in Paris had come to regard Algeria and the Algerians as part of France, and Algerian territory was divided into the same type of administrative subdivisions, called departments, as France was. Algerians of European origin or people of North African ancestry who had adopted the language and culture of France could vote in French elections to select representatives for the Chamber of Deputies in Paris.

Another factor in France's decision to resist the Algerian nationalists was its defeat in Indochina (what is now Vietnam, Cambodia, and Laos), a defeat that had been sealed the same year the struggle over Algeria began. The French military felt humiliated by its loss to the Viet Minh. Officers vowed to never suffer such a humiliation again. These officers believed that they had learned important lessons about how to fight an unconventional war from their experiences in Southeast Asia. Once the fighting in Algeria started, they decided to put these lessons to good use.

They did. French forces in Algeria were able to seal the country's borders and defeat the guerrilla insurgency of the Algerian National Liberation Front (Front de Libération Nationale, or FLN). They were much less successful in dealing with the campaign of urban terrorism that the FLN waged in Algiers, Oran, and other principal cities. Despite using torture as a tool in interrogating FLN suspects, the French police and

The Battle of Algiers

Terrorism against European civilians—bombings, shootings, and selective assassinations of notable political figures—figured prominently in the war, especially in Algeria, but in metropolitan France as well. The FLN [National Liberation Front] generally acknowledged that this activity was terrorism, although of course justifiable. It was intended to compel the French government to accede to demands as well as to reinforce the authority of the FLN within the nationalist movement and its legitimacy in the eyes of audiences in Algeria, France, and the world. In France, violence against the French and their property was meant to "bring the war home."*

---

* Martha Crenshaw. "Terrorism in the Algerian War" in Martha Crenshaw (ed.), *Terrorism in Context.* University Park, PA: Pennsylvania State University Press, 1995, p. 485.

military forces were unable to stop the FLN from assassinating French policemen and setting off bombs in neighborhoods inhabited by Europeans.

The latter infuriated the European settler population, whose spokesmen demanded a harsh crackdown. French forces responded to this pressure not only by seeking to dismantle the FLN's terrorist apparatus but also by carrying out measures against the local Algerian Muslim population more generally. This had the unintended effect of provoking the anger of this population and winning new recruits for the FLN. It also made the FLN far more popular among members of the Muslim community than it would have been otherwise. To some extent, then, the French did the FLN's work for the group.

Eventually, in 1958, the European settlers and elements of the French military in Algeria became so frustrated by their inability to defeat the insurgency that they demanded that a government of national emergency be appointed in Paris— on the threat of their staging an insurrection of their own. Parliament complied and appointed General Charles de Gaulle as new chief of state. The settlers were elated, believing that de Gaulle was a strong defender of *Algérie française,* or continued French rule in Algeria. This turned out not to be the case. De Gaulle's government opened negotiations with the FLN in the following year. These discussions led to complete Algerian independence in 1962.

There was a backlash during the negotiations. Infuriated at what they regarded as de Gaulle's betrayal, some of the settlers and army officers organized their own terrorist apparatus, the Secret Army Organization (OAS). The OAS set off bombs in places where Muslims were known to congregate in Algiers and Oran. They also staged bank robberies and kidnappings for ransom in metropolitan France in order to finance their operations. The most spectacular of the OAS's plans were a series of what proved to be unsuccessful attempts to assassinate de Gaulle. All this violence was to no avail.

Despite Algeria, Palestine, and a handful of other cases, terrorism was not the major problem or central concern of governments around the world as it is today. The transformation of terrorism into the dramatic and global threat it poses in contemporary times is the result of events that unfolded during the 1960s. What occurred in those years that ushered in what some have called the "age of terrorism"?

CHAPTER 5

THE AGE OF TERRORISM BEGINS:
THE THIRD WAVE

Terrorism became a central concern for governments around the world during the second half of the 1960s. By and large, it had played a minor role during the national liberation struggles of the 1940s and 1950s and in Communist revolutionary activity in the same years. The revolution in China under Mao Tse-tung, for example, had succeeded without the benefit of much terrorism. In the 1960s, however, events occurred that pushed terrorism toward center stage, to a place where it captured the attention of the mass media on a worldwide basis. What happened? What caused it to happen?

CAUSES OF MODERN TERRORISM
Part of the answer has to do with changing technology. Thanks to the

satellite transmission of television pictures, it became possible for audiences around the world to watch live images of events as they occurred on the opposite side of the globe. International travel became faster and easier, thanks largely to the introduction of jetliners into commercial use (the Boeing 707 became the most commonly used aircraft in this period). The major airlines all published schedules that described when their flights would depart and when these flights were likely to arrive at their destinations. These developments made the lives of passengers easier, but it also made planning easier for would-be terrorists who wished to disrupt them.

In addition to these and other technological developments (such as the miniaturization of some weapons), a number of events occurred during the 1960s that appeared to prompt the radicalization of politics throughout much of the world and also helped initiate a "new age" of terrorism. Let us consider some of the most important events.

First and probably foremost was the Vietnam War, or rather the United States' involvement in it. Beginning in 1964–1965, large numbers of American troops were sent to South Vietnam in order to defend that country against an insurgency undertaken by the Viet Cong and their ally and sponsor, the Communist government of North Vietnam. The ultimately unsuccessful effort to protect the South from this insurgency ignited massive protests throughout much of the Western world: Many thousands of students took to the streets to protest this American effort to repress, as they saw it, a heroic struggle by a third world people to achieve national liberation.

Another development had particular repercussions throughout the Middle East. Over a period of six days in June 1967, the armed forces of Israel inflicted a devastating and humiliating defeat on Egypt, Jordan, and Syria. Palestinian groups who had hoped that a war between Israel and its neighbors would bring about the destruction of Israel were bitterly disappointed. Israel emerged as the victor, and its victory included the conquest of the West Bank, East Jerusalem, the Gaza Strip, the Sinai Desert, and the Golan Heights. In short, the Palestinian goal of destroying the state of Israel and replacing it with a Palestinian one appeared more remote than ever. How could this objective now be achieved?

Third, the winds of revolutionary change were blowing in Latin America throughout the 1960s. During the first half of the decade, many Latin American revolutionaries, often young university students, looked to the example set by Fidel Castro in Cuba. Castro and his followers in the Sierra Maestra Mountains had used guerrilla warfare to defeat the highly unpopular dictatorship of Fulgencio Batista in 1959. Castro had described cities as the "graveyards of revolution," and in the years after Castro's success, guerrilla bands took to the mountains and jungles of various Latin American countries hoping to duplicate Castro's achievement. Foremost of these efforts was that of Ernesto "Che" Guevara. Guevara had been one of the leaders of the Cuban revolution; he hoped to lead his own revolution against the Bolivian government from the slopes of the Andes.

Neither Guevara nor the efforts of the other revolutionary guerrillas succeeded. Guevara and his band were hunted down and destroyed by the Bolivian army in 1967. Guevara was killed in the process. At this point, Latin America's numerous Marxist revolutionaries were in search of some alternative means of bringing down the military dictatorships and the weak and often corrupt democratic regimes that dominated the continent.

A final precursor to the "age of terrorism" was the Sino–Soviet split. Mao Tse-tung, the leader of Communist China, repeatedly accused his counterparts in the Soviet Union of betraying the revolutionary cause by seeking "peaceful coexistence" and later "détente" with the United States and the other capitalist countries. Mao accused them of becoming "revisionists," a Marxist-Leninist heresy. "Revisionists" were Marxists who believed that the goal of socialism could be achieved by peaceful means once workers had acquired the right to vote under democratic circumstances. In 1966, Mao unleashed the Great Proletarian Cultural Revolution, a massive effort to preserve the revolutionary enthusiasm of the Chinese people through verbal and physical attacks on public officials and party bureaucrats.

One of the effects of Mao's hard-line approach to the Marxist-Leninist revolutionary cause was a split in the Communist movement throughout the world. In Europe, Latin America, and elsewhere, pro-Mao factions split away from the major pro-Soviet Communist parties and created their own organizations. These pro-Mao organizations, such as the Communist Party of Peru: Marxist-Leninist, often included cadres (core groups of leaders) that were thoroughly committed to making a violent revolution in their own countries.

These conditions, both physical and human, provided the background for the outbreaks of terrorist violence that occurred throughout much of the world during the late 1960s and 1970s. Little of this third wave of terrorism was driven by religious considerations. Unlike the terrorism at the end of the twentieth century and in the first decade of the twenty-first, religious fundamentalism was not a central factor.

TERRORIST GROUPS OF THE THIRD WAVE

Within the advanced industrialized democracies, including the United States, the terrorist groups that appeared in the late 1960s and after expressed commitments to either an ideological or a nationalist cause. Those that claimed inspiration from the revolutionary ideology tended, with a few exceptions, to be weak and relatively short-lived. Japan had its Japanese Red Army, France its Direct Action, Great Britain its Angry Brigade, and the United States its Weather Underground and Symbionese Liberation Army. Despite their claims to being "armies" replete with commandants and generals, these were typically small, isolated bands of people capable of bombing, kidnapping, and killing on a limited basis. Their leaders' inflated rhetoric about worldwide revolution typically masked their own weakness.

In a few industrialized democracies, including Germany (or what was then called West Germany) and Italy, revolutionary left terrorism was more substantial. Spain, Northern Ireland, Latin America, and Palestine also had recognized terrorist incidents.

Germany

By the late 1960s, West Germany possessed one of the world's most prosperous economies. In term of politics, the country had overcome its Nazi past and had undergone a highly successful transition to constitutional democracy both on paper and in the minds of most of its citizens. On the surface, West Germany did not seem like fertile soil for serious terrorist activity. This turned out not to be the case.

Beginning in the late 1960s and continuing for more than a decade thereafter, the Rote Armee Fraktion (Red Army Faction, also called the Baader-Meinhof Gang); Bewegung 2 Juni (Movement 2 June); and a few smaller groups waged a terrorist campaign against German capitalism and what they regarded as the "fascist" character of the Bonn Republic. Bankers, businessmen, and politicians (including the mayor of West Berlin) were assassinated or kidnapped. Banks were robbed, and bombs set off. The revolutionary terrorists developed links to some of the Palestinian organizations, the Marxist Popular Front for the Liberation of Palestine (PFLP) in particular. They staged joint operations, including taking the Organization of Petroleum Exporting Countries (OPEC) oil ministers hostage in Vienna in 1976 and skyjacking an Air France jetliner bound from Paris to Tel Aviv later in the year (the Entebbe Incident). The German groups were also the beneficiaries of some assistance from the Eastern European Soviet bloc states, who were interested in causing trouble within the North Atlantic Treaty Organization (NATO) alliance.

Left-wing terrorism in Germany at first declined and then came to an end with the capture of most of those involved. Of equal importance were the collapse of the entire Communist enterprise with the disintegration of the Soviet bloc in 1989 and the implosion of the Soviet Union itself two years later.

Italy

Ideologically motivated terrorist activity in Italy was even more substantial than in Germany. It lasted longer, involved more people—both as perpetrators and victims (300 were killed and thousands injured)—and included not only left-wing revolutionary groups but also right-wing neo-fascist bands as well.

Between 1969 and 1983, Italians experienced what many came to describe as the "years of lead," an almost 15-year period when the streets and public squares in Italy's major cities were often filled with the sounds of gunfire and the explosion of bombs. Left-wing revolutionary organizations such as the Red Brigades and Front Line launched terrorist campaigns aimed at ending capitalism and bringing down the country's seriously

The Italian Red Brigades

Without doubt the most significant event in the Red Brigades' attempt to disarticulate the Italian state began on March 16, 1978, when Aldo Moro, the former prime minister and pre-eminent Christian Democratic leader, was abducted. Moro was taken from his automobile on the Via Fani in Rome by a brigade from the Red Brigades' Roman Column. This was done after they had killed his driver and police bodyguards. On May 10, 55 days later, Moro's body was found in the trunk of an abandoned car left in the middle of Rome, approximately halfway between the national headquarters of the Christian Democrats and the Italian Communist Party.*

The symbolism was not lost on the country's fractious politicians.

---

* Leonard Weinberg and William L. Eubank. *The Rise and Fall of Italian Terrorism*. Boulder, CO: Westview Press, 1987, p. 69.

flawed but nonetheless democratic system of government. Emerging from the mass student-led protest movements of the 1960s, the revolutionary terrorist groups kidnapped and shot many businessmen, judges, and politicians, including the former prime minister Aldo Moro, in their efforts to topple the system that they had come to despise.

Unlike the situation in Germany, however, there was also a significant amount of terrorist activity coming from the far right. Neo-fascist groups that called themselves the New Order, National Vanguard, National Front, National Action, and Mussolini Action Squads detonated bombs in banks, on trains, in railroad station waiting rooms, and at outdoor rallies. They killed hundreds during these *stragi*, or massacres. The purpose behind these bombings was to prevent Italy from "going Red" or becoming Communist (during the 1970s, Italy had the largest Communist party in the Western world, so their fears were not completely unfounded). The neo-fascists hoped that the violence would create such turmoil and uncertainty that the Italian public would support a seizure of power by antidemocratic elements in the military and national security agencies.

In the long run, neither the terrorism of the left revolutionaries nor that of the right-wing neo-fascist groups succeeded. By using a combination of force and guile, the Italian authorities were able to arrest, prosecute, and imprison many of the terrorists. Those willing to inform on their confederates were offered leniency and opportunities to return to normal lives.

Spain

Political ideology was not the only force at work in promoting terrorism in Western Europe during the 1960s and 1970s. Nationalism was another. Until the mid-1970s, Spain was ruled by the dictatorship of Francisco Franco. Franco and his government were committed to preventing any manifestations of regional autonomy, particularly on the part of the Basque population that lived in the northwestern part of the country.

Virtually all expressions of Basque cultural distinctiveness were barred by the government in Madrid. It was against this background that a group that called itself Euskadi Ta Askatasuna (ETA, or Basque Homeland and Freedom) emerged. After some years of study during the 1960s, ETA embarked on a terrorist campaign aimed at achieving independence for the Basque areas. During these early years, ETA largely confined itself to killing representatives of Spanish authority; members of the civil guards (a national police force) were frequent targets. The most spectacular attack was its assassination of Franco's second in command and likely successor, Admiral Luis Carrero Blanco, in Madrid in 1972.

Franco died in 1975, and the country he had ruled for a quarter-century underwent a transition to democracy. The new Spanish constitution provided for formation of the Basque Autonomous Community with its own elected regional legislature and cultural freedom. These developments did not bring an end to ETA violence, however. Complete independence was still its goal. Today, halfway through the first decade of the twenty-first century, the ETA continues to carry out terrorist attacks throughout Spain.

Northern Ireland

The status of Catholics in Northern Ireland also became a source of terrorism in the late 1960s. Northern Ireland is the section of the island that retained its tie to the United Kingdom after the establishment of an independent Republic of Ireland in the years after World War I. Ulster, or Northern Ireland, including the cities of Belfast and Londonderry, has a Protestant majority community. Many members of this community strongly opposed a united Ireland and rule from Dublin because they feared domination by a Catholic community that would have a large majority if the land were to be unified.

In Northern Ireland, which had its own provincial government, Catholics suffered from a variety of forms of economic

In 1998, the Real IRA carried out a car bombing in Omagh, Ulster, a Protestant area that opposes a united Ireland. The attack was particularly deadly because the terrorists had phoned in a false tip to the police, causing authorities to direct civilians away from the fake location and to the actual site of the bombing.

hardships and political discrimination. They were also humiliated every summer when Protestant groups celebrated their community's military defeat of Catholic forces at the end of the seventeenth century by staging provocative marches through Catholic sections of the major cities. The result of these practices was the emergence of a Catholic civil rights movement in 1967–1968. Modeling their behavior along the lines of the American civil rights movement, Catholics staged marches and protests demanding an end to discrimination. What began as peaceful demonstrations quickly escalated into violent confrontations between Catholics and Protestants.

On the Catholic, or republican, side, the long-standing Irish Republican Army (IRA) underwent a split. One faction of the IRA, the Provisionals or Provos, advocated the use of violence not only to defend the Catholic community but also to achieve the unification of Ulster with the Republic of Ireland to the south. On the other side of the ethnic and religious divide, the Protestant-dominated police forces, aided by "volunteers" from the Protestant patriotic societies, repeatedly used excessive force against Catholics in their efforts to repress what they feared was becoming an open rebellion.

In this context in 1972, the British government decided to send in the regular army to maintain public order because the violence on both sides had begun to spiral out of control. The Provisional IRA seized on this decision to argue that Northern Ireland was now under foreign occupation, and London would use all forms of violence to suppress all legitimate attempts to achieve a united Ireland.

The result of these developments was a quarter-century of what observers often refer to as "The Troubles." During this period, more than 3,000 people died as the result of terrorist attacks staged by both the IRA and Protestant paramilitary bands. The latter, often identified as "loyalists," were committed to maintaining the Protestant-dominated status quo.

Eventually, in 1998, negotiators of the British and Irish governments and representatives of the Catholic and Protestant communities in Northern Ireland were able to reach the Good Friday Agreement, or the Belfast Agreement. Among other things, this agreement provided for a power-sharing arrangement for a new elective regional government and for the "decommissioning" of the IRA's extensive stockpile of weapons. Irish voters then went to the polls and voted by a substantial majority to approve the agreement. Hopes were raised that peace was finally at hand. As of 2005, however, the agreement still had not been completely implemented. As a result, there is fear on both sides that terrorist activities might resume.

Latin America

Nationalism was not a major cause of terrorism in Latin America during the 1960s, 1970s, and later; ideology was. After the failure of several rural guerrilla campaigns to install Marxist regimes in Bolivia, Venezuela, and elsewhere (see previous sections) in the style of the Cuban revolution, terrorist groups who hoped to achieve the same end but by different means emerged in a number of Latin American countries.

Brazil, Uruguay, Argentina, and Colombia were the sites of particularly serious terrorist campaigns waged by Marxist insurgents. Unlike their counterparts in Western Europe, though, Latin America's "urban guerrillas," as they preferred to be known, often combined terrorist attacks in the major cities with at least fledgling attempts at low-intensity insurgencies in the countryside.

At the time, the Tupamaros were the most widely known of the "urban guerrilla" organizations. They became active in Uruguay, one of the continent's few stable democracies, in the late 1960s. Initially, the Tupamaros sought to win popular support among the slum dwellers of Montevideo by appearing to be Robin Hoods, stealing from the rich and giving to the poor. Early in their campaign, they carried out an armed robbery of a gambling casino, relieving some of its wealthy patrons of their cash and jewelry. The Tupamaros then distributed the proceeds of their stickup to the poor.

Another tactic that they employed was later copied by revolutionary organizations in other Latin American and Western European countries. It involved the kidnapping of prominent bankers, businessmen, and politicians. The Tupamaros would seize their victims, take them to a safe house, and then subject them to a mock trial before a "people's tribunal." Videotapes or transcripts of these "trials," at which the kidnapping victims were compelled to confess their crimes against the workers, were then distributed to the mass media. Usually, the victims were then released.

Eventually, the Tupamaros overplayed their hand. Their leaders came to believe that they were more powerful than they truly were. As a result, the Tupamaros began to stage attacks on the police and military. Uruguay's military was willing to permit the civilian government to deal with the problem—up to a point. When the Tupamaros began to kill members of the country's armed forces, the military leaders decided to act. In 1972, they staged a coup d'état and replaced the democratic government with a military regime. Acting under a state of emergency, the military, unrestrained by due process of law requirements, proceeded to destroy the Tupamaros. Some of its leaders were killed; others fled into exile. The organization's terrorist campaign was brought to an end.

Brutal repression also seemed to work in Brazil and Argentina, the two largest countries in South America. Brazil was ruled by a military dictatorship when a handful of revolutionary urban guerrilla groups began to stage terrorist attacks in 1967–1968. After these groups achieved some limited successes, which involved bank robberies and the kidnapping of bankers, businessmen, and foreign diplomats, the military took off their proverbial "kid gloves." Among other things, they tortured suspected terrorists into disclosing the whereabouts of their confederates, the leaders in particular. Within a relatively short time, virtually all terrorist activity in Brazil had come to an end.

The situation in Argentina was more complicated, but its outcome was virtually the same. Revolutionary organizations, including the Montoneros and the People's Revolutionary Army, limited their terrorist attacks during the presidency of widely popular Juan Perón. After Perón's death in 1973, they resumed the violence at a higher level than before his election. Finally, in 1976, the military seized power and launched a "dirty war" (1976–1982) aimed at purging Argentina of all traces of urban guerrilla activity. During this time, military personnel used extra-legal means—arbitrary arrests, illegal detention, torture, secret executions—to eliminate all those thought to support the cause of left-wing revolution. The country's ruling military junta succeeded in this task. The price that Argentina had to pay for this success was a high one: Members of the country's army and navy grabbed suspected terrorists, along with people suspected of sympathizing with their cause, off the streets without benefit of formal arrest. These detainees were then imprisoned, tortured, and often killed. Thousands died in this way before the military returned to its barracks and permitted Argentina to resume democratic rule.

Terrorism in Latin America did not come to an end with the defeat of its principal perpetrators in Uruguay, Brazil, and Argentina. In 1980, a new group, the Sendero Luminoso, or Shining Path, surfaced in Peru. The group has suffered a number of important setbacks, but its activities have continued. Likewise in Colombia, one of the world's most violent countries, the Revolutionary Armed Forces of Colombia (FARC) has persisted in its campaign of violence, sometimes in collaboration with the country's leading cocaine dealers, into the first decade of the twenty-first century.

Palestine

In the Middle East, Palestinian organizations were confronted by critical problems after the defeat of the conventional military forces of the Arab nations by the Israelis in June 1967. Before the Six-Day War, the Palestinians had hoped to provoke just such a confrontation between Israel and the Soviet-backed governments in Cairo and Damascus. When the smoke cleared, the Palestinians were even further from their goal of destroying Israel than they had been before the fighting. What to do?

In the aftermath of the war, the various Palestinian groups coalesced under an umbrella, or roof, organization, the Palestine Liberation Organization (PLO). Yasir Arafat, the leader of Fatah, the largest of the groups, became the PLO chairman. Under his leadership, in 1968, the PLO produced a new charter that called for the replacement of Israel by a "democratic secular state" of Palestine. The only way to achieve this secular state was by means of "armed struggle." No negotiations were possible, nor could the PLO depend on the Arab states to do its work for it. The PLO itself was to wage the "armed struggle."

At first, the PLO groups, borrowing from the Viet Cong, sought to wage guerrilla war. Operating from bases in Jordan, PLO groups launched attacks against Israeli targets in the West Bank, territory that the Israelis captured during the June 1967 fighting. These cross-border raids had very limited success. Among other problems, the rocky and often barren terrain on much of the West Bank did not lend itself to sustained guerrilla operations. The Jordanian government, led by King Hussein, was not pleased either, especially when the Israelis began to retaliate against Palestinian targets inside its territory.

As a result, some of the PLO-affiliated groups, notably the Popular Front for the Liberation of Palestine (PFLP), began to carry out terrorist attacks not only in the Middle East but in Europe as well. The most spectacular of these early terrorist events was the 1970 skyjacking of several passenger-filled jumbo jets from the skies over Western Europe and their forced landing at an airstrip in the Jordanian desert. After some days of negotiation between the PFLP and the Jordanian authorities, the skyjackers blew up the planes after the passengers had been safely transported to hotels in Amman.

After this widely publicized event (a picture of the planes exploding made the cover of *Life* and other Western magazines), the Jordanian government succeeded in expelling the PLO from the country. Arafat and the leaders of the other PLO-related groups then moved their bases of operation to Lebanon. From fall 1970 until their expulsion from Beirut in 1982, the PLO groups waged a terrorist campaign against Israel and those it presumed were Israel's friends.

First, the PLO groups carried out attacks against civilians inside Israel itself. In most of these cases, PLO bands crossed the Lebanese border and launched attacks on farming communities and small villages in northern Israel. In one case, they seized control of a middle school filled with students and killed many of the children as Israeli forces attempted to rescue them. In another, PLO fighters took control of the children's nursery at a kibbutz (an Israeli collective farm) and killed several infants and their adult caregivers before the authorities could intervene.

Sometimes the PLO was able to use surrogates from sympathetic groups elsewhere. In 1972, three members of the Japanese Red Army who had trained at a PFLP camp in Yemen took a commercial flight from Paris that landed at Lod Airport in Israel. Once on the tarmac, they took out the guns they had concealed in their carry-on bags and shot and killed two dozen Puerto Rican pilgrims who had come to visit the Christian holy sites.

Second, in addition to attacks inside Israel, the PLO also carried out "operations" against Israeli targets elsewhere. In September 1972, members of Black September, a PLO group, took over the Israeli athletes' dormitory at the summer Olympic Games in Munich, Germany. About a dozen athletes were killed, some during the initial break-in, others in the ensuing shootout between the terrorists and German police sharpshooters at the Munich airport. On another occasion, a PLO band appeared at an El-Al departure gate at Malpensa Airport outside Milan and shot the passengers waiting to board a flight to Israel.

Third, the citizens of countries the PLO regarded as simply sympathetic to Israel were also targeted for attack. Americans were among the favorites not only because of the sympathy but also because the United States was the home of television and other major channels of mass communication. In 1972, a PLO group took over the Saudi embassy in Addis Ababa, Ethiopia, and shot the American ambassador and his deputy to death when its demands were not met. The targets did not have to be American. On another occasion, PLO fighters skyjacked a German Lufthansa airliner over the Mediterranean and had it flown to Mogadishu, Somalia. The fighters threatened to kill all the passengers unless members of a German terrorist group awaiting trial in a German prison were released.

The PLO was not beyond attacking targets in the Arab world that its leaders regarded as hostile to their interests. In 1973, PLO fighters assassinated the Jordanian foreign minister as he emerged from his hotel in Cairo while on an official visit to Egypt. In Lebanon, the PLO carried out attacks on members of that country's Maronite (Christian) community before the organization's expulsion from the country in 1982.

In the late 1980s, with its headquarters relocated to Tunis in North Africa, the PLO expressed a willingness to suspend its terrorist attacks in exchange for open diplomatic discussions with the United States. Nonetheless, PLO terrorism continued, although at a reduced level, until it entered into the Oslo Accords with Israel in 1994. These accords provided for mutual recognition and final peace negotiations. Since then, PLO terrorism has risen and fallen with the fortunes of the "peace process," and its role as the principal perpetrator of Middle Eastern terrorism has been overtaken by other organizations. These newer organizations have claimed inspiration less from secular ideas about nationalism and social justice and more from strong religious convictions. In fact, these convictions have given rise to a fourth wave of modern terrorism, the so-called "new terrorism."

CHAPTER 6

THE NEW TERRORISM:
THE FOURTH WAVE

Two questions about what many observers have labeled "new terrorism" must be answered. First, when did it start? Second, how is it different from the terrorism of the 1960s and 1970s—or, what is new about the new terrorism?

ORIGIN OF NEW TERRORISM

Two major events served to ignite the worldwide wave of terrorist violence that has dominated the headlines during the last decades of the twentieth century and the first years of the twenty-first. The first event was the Iranian revolution of 1978–1979. Until millions of Iranians poured into the streets of Tehran and the country's other major cities to demand the end of monarchy, many observers had come to believe that the era of mass social revolutions had come to an end. Furthermore, everyone knew or thought that they knew what twentieth-century revolutions were all about. Modern revolutions were undertaken in the name of Marx, Lenin, and Mao, the key figures of the Russian and Chinese revolutions. Virtually all of the major revolutions of the nineteenth and twentieth centuries had had an antireligious tone, with the revolutionaries believing that organized religion represented a barrier to the kinds of changes they intended to make in their respective countries.

In these and other ways, the Iranian revolution was unexpected. Not only did it involve millions of people, but its leaders were not Marxists of one kind or another but mullahs and ayatollahs, members of Iran's Shi'ite clergy. To the extent that the Iranian king, Muhammad Reza Shah Pahlavi, and his American allies worried about revolution, their worries were directed toward the Iranian Communist Party as well as the fact that the country shared a long border with the Soviet Union.

It came as a surprise that the key figure in forcing the shah to leave Iran at the beginning of 1979 was the austere 77-year-old Ayatollah Ruhollah Khomeini. More than anything else, Khomeini's religiously grounded condemnations of the shah's luxurious lifestyle, the corruption of his court, his close ties to the infidel United States, and the anti-Islamic nature of the system over which he reigned had the greatest impact.

In place of the corrupt and highly unpopular monarchy, the ayatollah and his followers established an Islamic republic in which bands of Revolutionary Guards sought to impose a kind of puritanical way of life on their fellow citizens, a life based on the religious judgments of the country's mullahs. Serious punishments awaited those who strayed too far from the straight path.

The creation of an intensely anti-American and anti-Israeli Islamic fundamentalist regime in Iran had a dramatic impact on the countries of the Middle East that had significant Shi'ite

Ayatollah Khomeini is shown here waving to a crowd of enthusiastic supporters in Tehran. The revolution that led to the unseating of the Iranian shah placed Khomeini in power and enabled the establishment of a fundamentalist Islamic regime.

populations, such as Lebanon. In these countries, new groups with names like Al-Da'wa and Amal, which were committed to transforming their countries into Iran-style theocracies and radically reducing American influence, appeared.

Shi'ites represent a distinct minority of Muslims around the world. The majority of Muslims are Sunnis. An event that had the same type of radicalizing influence on members of the latter denomination as the Iranian revolution had for many Shi'ites occurred. This event, also in 1979, was the decision of leaders of the Soviet Union to invade Afghanistan, a Muslim country with a largely Sunni population.

A Communist government had come to power in Kabul, the Afghan capital, and had sought to impose a number of highly unpopular social and economic changes. The various tribal communities into which the country's population was divided launched a rebellion aimed at overthrowing the Communist regime. When the insurrection appeared to be on the verge of success, the Red Army was sent into Afghanistan in order to rescue the Communist regime. For many Muslims around the world, the intervention was interpreted as an invasion of the House of Islam by godless Communists. The proper response was a holy war, or *jihad*, aimed at driving out the infidels.

Clerics throughout the Muslim world issued appeals for believers to go to Afghanistan and drive out the invaders. Both Saudi Arabia and the United States (sensing that the Soviets had gotten mired in a quagmire) provided money and equipment in order to help train "holy warriors" to expel the Soviet forces. The jihad succeeded. The Afghan militias, aided by the largely Arab holy warriors, forced Gorbachev and other Kremlin decision-makers to withdraw the Red Army in 1988. Without the Red Army's support, the Communist regime in Kabul quickly collapsed.

Among the Arabs who answered the appeal for holy war were a wealthy Saudi businessman by the name of Osama bin Laden and an Egyptian physician, Dr. Ayman al-Zawahiri, who had been imprisoned because of his involvement in the successful Islamic Jihad plot to assassinate Egyptian president Anwar Sadat in 1981. Bin Laden and al-Zawahiri formed the nucleus of what the world soon came to know as al Qaeda, the most destructive and complex terrorist organization in history.

The Iranian revolution and the jihad in Afghanistan during the 1980s were the principal events that have given rise to what many refer to as "new terrorism." Before the continuing development of this most recent wave of terrorist violence is traced, what makes new terrorism new should be addressed.

ASPECTS OF NEW TERRORISM

First, and most obviously, the practitioners of the new terrorism are religiously motivated. In many, although not all, cases, they are "Islamists," a minority of Muslims who believe that the teachings of their religion require them to use violence to topple what they regard as the un-Islamic governments in Algeria, Egypt, Saudi Arabia, and elsewhere in the Middle East. These Islamists also intend to remove all Western, mainly American, influence from the House of Islam. In their campaigns of violence, the Islamists believe that they are acting on behalf of the divine and will be rewarded for doing so.

Second, unlike the secular terrorists of the 1960s and 1970s, who wanted a "lot of people watching, not a lot of people dead,"[12] the religiously driven new terrorists want to inflict mass casualties on those they regard as their enemies. In killing many, today's Islamist terrorists believe that they are carrying out the will of God, not acting on behalf of some secular ideology or mundane territorial goal.

Related to this divinely-inspired lack of restraint, contemporary terrorists have shown an interest in acquiring and using weapons of mass destruction (WMD): chemical, biological, radiological, and nuclear weapons. This interest has not been confined exclusively to Islamist groups. Other religiously-inspired terrorists have also sought and, on occasion, used them. The most notable example to date was the Japanese religious cult Aum Shinrikyo ("Supreme Truth"). In 1995, members of Aum Shinrikyo dispersed deadly nerve gas in the Tokyo subway system during rush hour in an effort to kill thousands and, they hoped, ignite a new world war. Members of this religious group managed to kill only a dozen commuters before the authorities were able to stop the mayhem and arrest the perpetrators.

A final way in which the new terrorism differs from older versions is the extensive use of suicide bombers. During the 1960s and 1970s, most terrorists hoped to live again to fight another day. Beginning in Lebanon in the early 1980s and continuing to this day, however, the world has witnessed a series of terrorist campaigns in which the principal tactic of those waging them has been suicide bombing, attacks in which the person carrying out the attack either drives a bomb-laden car or truck at a particular target or has explosives strapped to his or her body and then detonates them once at a designated place. This tactic has become widely used not only by Islamist groups but also by other terrorist organizations in South Asia and elsewhere.

Lebanon

The Iranian revolution and the subsequent creation of a radical Islamic republic in what had been a pro-American monarchy excited Shi'ite populations throughout the Middle East. This was true in Iraq under Saddam Hussein as well as in the various oil-rich sheikdoms and emirates scattered along the southern shore of the Persian Gulf. The revolution had its most powerful impact in Lebanon.

At the time of the revolution, Lebanon was embroiled in a bitter civil war, one that pitted one religious or ethnic group

Hizbollah in Lebanon and Islamist Terrorism

"If America kills my people, then my people must kill Americans," Musawi said later. "We have already said that if self-defense and if the stand against American, Israeli and French oppression constitutes terrorism, then we are terrorists in that context. This path is the path of blood, the path of martyrdom. For us death is easier than smoking a cigarette if it comes while fighting for the cause of God and while defending the oppressed."*

---

* Hizbollah leader Hussein Musawi, quoted in Robin Wright, *Sacred Terror: The Wrath of Militant Islam*. New York: Simon & Schuster, 1986, pp. 83–84.

against another. The Shi'ites were Lebanon's single largest religious community, but also the one with the least economic and political power. In other words, it was a community with long-standing grievances against the prevailing system. These resentments had given rise to Amal, an organization committed to advancing the interests of the community largely through peaceful means. Within two years of the Ayatollah Khomeini's coming to power in Iran, Shi'ites in Lebanon underwent a process of radicalization.

In 1982, the Israelis invaded Lebanon with the intent of eliminating the PLO presence. A short time after the Israelis marched on Beirut, the Iranian government sent a detachment of Revolutionary Guards to the Bekaa Valley in eastern Lebanon to train young Lebanese Shi'ites to fight the Israelis and the Christian groups struggling to retain their hold on power.

Because of the breakdown of central government authority in Beirut and the atrocities caused by the civil war and the continuing Israeli presence, the United States, France, and Italy sent peacekeeping forces to Lebanon in 1983. Rather than retaining their neutrality, the American and French forces became identified with the Christian cause in the ongoing civil war. Shi'ites who lived in the slums of South Beirut saw themselves as the targets of the American and French military presence. Against this background, Hizbollah (the Party of God) was created under the auspices of the Iranian Revolutionary Guard. Hizbollah, an expression of Shi'ite militancy, soon embarked on a terrorist campaign aimed at getting the Americans, French, and Israelis to leave Lebanon. Its most widely publicized terrorist attacks were the suicide bombings of the American and French embassies in Beirut and the American Marine Corps barracks near the city's international airport in December 1983. These suicide attacks worked in the sense that both the American and French governments decided to withdraw their forces rather than face mounting casualties. Eventually, the Israelis followed suit.

Palestine

Israel itself became the target of religiously inspired terrorism at the end of the 1980s. The PLO and the various groups from which it was composed had carried out terrorist attacks on Israeli targets for years (see previous sections). The PLO, however, was essentially a nationalist organization, some of whose militants were originally Marxists (the now-defunct Soviet Union was a major supporter) and pan-Arab nationalists. When a popular uprising against Israeli control of the West Bank and the Gaza Strip (the intifada) broke out in December 1987, new groups appeared to challenge PLO leadership of the Palestinian cause.

Hamas and Palestinian Islamic Jihad (PIJ) appeared on the West Bank and in the Gaza Strip shortly after the beginning of the intifada. The roots of both groups were in the Egyptian Muslim Brotherhood, an Islamic fundamentalist organization of long standing. Over the next few years, Hamas and PIJ sought to transform the Palestinian struggle with Israel into a religious conflict, not around competing claims over land but around divine intent. No territorial compromises with the Jews, who had entered and seized control over part of the House of Islam, were possible, and in the effort to expel these infidels from this House, virtually any means were justified.

In practice, this meant the adoption of suicide bombing, as pioneered by Hizbollah, Hamas, and PIJ. Beginning in 1993 and continuing on and off since, both groups have employed "human bombs" in an effort to sow terror among Israelis and provide Palestinians with a sense of justifiable revenge.

In practice, the suicide bombers were typically young men of a religious bent who came forward and volunteered to sacrifice their lives on behalf of what they regarded as a holy cause. After a modest amount of spiritual and technical preparation, trainers sent these *shahids* (martyrs) on their way. They would cross into Israel from the West Bank or Gaza Strip with the aid of Palestinian "'guides" who were familiar with the area to be attacked. At this point, the shahid would board a public bus and, once the bus filled with passengers, explode the bomb strapped to his body; or, he would walk into a crowded shopping center or restaurant and do the same. Over the years, Israeli security services have improved their ability to block these attacks before they can be carried out, but their rate of success remains well below 100 percent.

Suicide bombings have come to be used by a number of terrorist groups around the world, including the Liberation Tigers of Tamil Eelam in Sri Lanka and the rebels in Chechnya. The organization with which the technique is most closely associated is al Qaeda, the world's most feared and most lethal terrorist organization.

Al Qaeda

Like Hamas and PIJ, the origins of al Qaeda ("the base") are found in Egypt, where a number of militant Islamic groups that grew out of the Muslim Brotherhood committed themselves to the overthrow of the corrupt secular government. Members of one of the groups managed to assassinate President Sadat in 1981; others launched murderous attacks on the country's Coptic Christian minority, public officials, and foreign tourists in the following years.

The Egyptian authorities responded to the threat by arresting many militants and forcing others to flee into exile. Among the latter was Ayman al-Zawahiri, a physician from a prominent Cairo family. In 1986, Dr. al-Zawahiri and other Egyptian militants went to the city of Peshawar on Pakistan's border with Afghanistan. Their purpose was to participate in the jihad aimed at expelling Soviet forces from Afghanistan. It was a fateful development.

There, al-Zawahiri met Osama bin Laden, a wealthy young Saudi who had also come to Peshawar to assist thousands of young Islamic volunteers from all over the world who had answered the call to jihad. Bin Laden and a religious leader,

Sheik Abdallah Azzam, had already organized a service bureau to help the young militants prepare for war in Afghanistan. Al-Zawahiri soon joined the leadership of this organization. Their efforts bore fruit: The fight in Afghanistan succeeded. Soviet forces were withdrawn in 1988, and the Communist regime in Kabul collapsed shortly after their departure.

At this point, bin Laden, al-Zawahiri, and the other leaders were filled with a sense of triumph and possibility. If a comparative handful of young militants could defeat and humiliate what had been considered the most or second-most powerful military in the world, the possibility of taking the holy war and holy warriors elsewhere became apparent. At this point and for this purpose, al Qaeda was organized by bin Laden, al-Zawahiri, Azzam, and a handful of others.

Within this group of leaders, opinions about where to strike next differed. Azzam wanted to encourage jihads, or holy wars, against the "near enemy," governments in largely Muslim countries or regions that had fallen into the hands of non-Muslims, such as the Philippines, Kashmir, and Palestine. Azzam and his two sons were murdered in Peshawar in 1989 by still-unidentified killers. As a result of their deaths, the views of bin Laden and al-Zawahiri prevailed. These views stressed the elimination of governments like that of Egypt, which was led by apostates—Muslims who in the eyes of these purists had strayed from "the straight path" laid down by the Prophet Mohammed. More ambitious still, there was talk of waging a worldwide jihad to restore the Muslim community to its former preeminence.

A key event in the evolution of al Qaeda was the Iraqi invasion of Kuwait in 1990. Next door, Saudi Arabia felt seriously threatened by the forces of Saddam Hussein. Osama bin Laden offered to bring his fighters, the "holy warriors," from Afghanistan to defend the kingdom against a possible attack. The Saudi royal family turned down his offer and instead turned to the United States for protection. This decision infuriated bin Laden. He was especially incensed that the Saudis would turn to infidels to defend the "land of the two holy sites" (Mecca and Medina). Bin Laden's criticism of this policy became so vocal that he was eventually expelled from Saudi Arabia and had his citizenship withdrawn by the government.

Later in 1990, bin Laden, al-Zawahiri, and many other figures in al Qaeda moved to Sudan. This North African country had recently fallen under the control of an Islamist government headed by a military figure, General Omar Hassan al-Bashir, and Hassan al-Turabi, a Paris-trained Islamist philosopher. Over the next few years, al Qaeda enjoyed the hospitality of the Sudanese government. For the most part, al Qaeda's efforts were directed against Egypt (President Mubarak was the target of an assassination attempt while on a visit to Addis Ababa, Ethiopia) and toward defending Muslims and Muslim interests in Bosnia, Kashmir, Chechnya, and the Philippines. The continued American military presence in Saudi Arabia and other places in the region proved to be a growing irritant. In 1991, when the United States sent forces to Somalia on a humanitarian mission under United Nations auspices, al Qaeda sent equipment and trainers to Mogadishu to help a local warlord drive out the Americans. In 1992, after the "Blackhawk Down" incident, in which the warlord's followers shot down two American helicopters, the Clinton administration ended the American presence there.

Based on this decision, the al Qaeda leadership drew the conclusion that the United States was a "paper tiger," meaning that, like the Soviet Union, it was far more formidable on paper that it was in reality, especially when challenged by holy warriors. The view that the United States was weak, weaker than the Soviets, combined with the organization's hostility to the American presence in the Middle East, led to al Qaeda's ultimate decision to wage a worldwide jihad against American power and America's friends and allies.

First, though, al Qaeda leaders had to cope with their expulsion from Sudan. In the period of 1995–1996, al Qaeda terrorists

Osama bin Laden and the group he helped to create, al Qaeda, have become synonymous with terrorism in the twenty-first century. Bin Laden is pictured here in a photograph from 1998.

not only attempted to assassinate Egyptian president Mubarak but also set off a series of bombs in Saudi Arabia. The governments affected by these attacks demanded that the Sudanese expel bin Laden and the other al Qaeda leaders. Under mounting international pressure, the government in Khartoum complied. In 1996, al Qaeda moved its base of operations back to Afghanistan, a country that had fallen under the Islamic fundamentalist rule of the Taliban.

In this hospitable setting, al Qaeda set up training camps to prepare young Islamic militants from all over the world, including Western Europe and the United States, to wage holy war. In 1998, bin Laden promoted the formation of the World Islamic Front for Jihad Against Jews and Crusaders. The Front then issued a fatwa, or religious decree, that urged all Muslims to kill Americans, civilians as well as military, wherever they could be found.

A series of spectacular terrorist attacks followed the issuance of this fatwa. The American embassies in Nairobi, Kenya, and Dar es Salaam, Tanzania, were bombed in 1998, leaving hundreds dead. The U.S.S. *Cole,* an American naval vessel, was bombed while resting at anchor in the port of Aden in October 2000; 17 sailors were killed. Other attacks, including a scheme to blow up the Los Angeles International Airport at the time of the new millennium in 2000, were foiled.

The most horrendous of al Qaeda's attacks was the September 11, 2001, assaults on the Twin Towers of the World Trade Center in New York and on the Pentagon. By seizing control of commercial airliners and crashing them into these buildings, al Qaeda suicide bombers managed to kill more than 3,000 civilians within the space of a few hours, the worst single terrorist event in history.

THE WAR ON TERRORISM

The immediate result of the 9/11 attacks was the decision by the Bush administration to launch a war on terrorism on a worldwide basis. In practical terms, the war on terrorism led to the successful effort by the U.S. military and various Afghan factions to overthrow the Taliban regime and close down al Qaeda's operations throughout Afghanistan. In the course of these operations in fall and winter of 2001–2002, many important al Qaeda figures were killed or captured. Some were seized in Pakistan; Pakistan's leader, President Pervez Musharraf, became the target of multiple assassination attempts because of his cooperation with the Americans.

The elimination of al Qaeda's sanctuary in Afghanistan has not brought an end to al Qaeda. Instead, the organization has become far more decentralized than it was before the 9/11 attacks. It continues to carry out attacks in conjunction with other radical Islamist groups in the Philippines, Indonesia, Morocco, Algeria, and, most of all, post-Saddam Iraq. From Bali, Indonesia (where one al Qaeda–linked group set off a bomb in a nightclub that killed close to a hundred tourists in 2002), to Madrid, Spain (where another Islamist cell detonated multiple bombs on board commuter trains as they reached the Atocha rail station on the morning of March 11, 2004, leaving almost 200 dead), the admirers and followers of Dr. al-Zawahiri and Osama bin Laden continue to pose a serious challenge to governments throughout much of the world. Civilians are in peril.

CONCLUSIONS:
DOES TERRORISM END?

The previous chapters were about the past and the present. Now, what about the future of political terrorism?

Will the current era of terrorism and the war on terror that it provoked come to an end? What will the future look like? The historical record, the one examined in the previous chapters, suggests that the answer to the first question is certainly "yes." The European anarchists of the nineteenth century and their "propaganda by deed" have long since departed the scene. The social revolutionary terrorism of the 1960s and 1970s has ended, for the most part. The groups in Germany, Italy, Argentina, Uruguay, and other Latin American countries that employed terrorism to advance the cause of Marx and Lenin have disappeared or, in the few cases where they have not, they have turned away from politics and toward organized crime. Making money from the production and distribution of cocaine and heroin, not the ignition of working-class revolution, has become their principal activity.

At present, the United States, Spain, Great Britain, and other democracies are challenged by Islamist groups that either belong to the al Qaeda network or are sympathetic to its aims. These groups claim to be waging a jihad against the enemies of Islam. By using suicide bombings and other forms of mass-casualty terrorism, they intend to drive the West, the United States in particular, out of the Middle East; topple the region's anti-Islamic governments (such as Egypt); and, most ambitiously, re-create the caliphate, the Muslim world as it existed during the Middle Ages.

What are their prospects? Will they succeed? The answer is, "probably not." The followers of the prophet Mohammed, who originally created the House of Islam in the seventh and eighth centuries A.D., did so by conquering territories in the Middle East, North Africa, and South Asia by conventional military means—powerful armies, not terrorism. (In the lands conquered by these armies—Egypt, for example—Christians and Jews were treated with considerable tolerance.) Likewise, during the period of the Christian Crusades, which began in the eleventh century A.D., it was not terrorism but regular armies that rallied to the cause and compelled the Crusaders to leave the region.

In other words, the historical record suggests that, to succeed, today's Islamic militants will have to do more than simply detonate bombs in public places in Riyadh, Saudi Arabia, or in New York. They would need to employ a large military force and then wage war accordingly. The only case to date where such a force was constituted was by the Taliban regime in Afghanistan. The latter's militia was defeated, and the regime itself driven from power after a series of skirmishes with U.S. Special Forces and northern Afghan tribal forces in 2001 in the months after the 9/11 attacks on the World Trade Center and the Pentagon. The Taliban had provided al Qaeda with sanctuary and aid, hence the U.S. invasion.

There have been a few cases in which militant Islamist terrorism has worked, at least on a limited basis. The Spanish government withdrew its military from Iraq after the March 11, 2004, bombings of commuter trains in Madrid. The Israeli government's decision to withdraw from southern Lebanon in 2000 is similar. In these instances and a few others, the governments involved did not have any serious national interests at stake. In circumstances in which such interests were involved, as with India's commitment to retaining control over Kashmir, for example, the terrorist campaigns did not achieve the objectives their perpetrators had hoped.

Many believe that the terrorist campaigns of Islamist groups and the war on terrorism being waged against them will continue for generations to come. Perhaps, but it must be remembered that periods of intense religious excitement tend to come and go. The waxing and waning of religious fundamentalism has been a regular feature of Hinduism, Judaism, the Ghost Dance religion of some Native American tribes, and Christianity over the centuries. The United States, for example, has experienced multiple "Great Awakenings" over the course of its history. These periods of religious excitement often were accompanied by bouts of violence directed against nonbelievers or more moderate elements within the community of believers.

The same may be said about the history of Islam. At the end of the nineteenth century, for example, an African tribal leader proclaimed himself the Mahdi—the Holy Redeemer— and sought to drive the British from Sudan. The capital city of Khartoum was captured, and the commander of British forces, Charles "Chinese" Gordon, was killed. Within a few years, however, the British were able to reverse the situation and defeat the Mahdi's holy warriors. The Mahdi and the enthusiasm he generated soon faded from the scene. Is there any reason to believe that something similar will not happen with al Qaeda and the various groups to which it is linked?

Unfortunately, to say that the current period of religiously driven terrorism will come to an end is not to say that terrorism itself will end. Terrorism is a tactic, not an ideology or religious practice. It may be used by a wide variety of groups with a wide variety of political aims. It is also a tactic that plays well on television and is easily adapted to Internet technology. The chances are that, in the future, followers of one cause or another will find it too attractive to ignore. The genie of terrorism is now out of the bottle.

If terrorism is likely to be with us for the foreseeable future, what means are its perpetrators likely to use? Observers who are willing to answer this question, including President George Bush and UN secretary-general Kofi Annan, often refer to the use of WMD. They believe that terrorist groups are not only willing but actively preparing to use chemical, biological, radiological, and even nuclear weapons in an effort to kill as

Aum Shinrikyo Attacks the Tokyo Subways

On March 20,1995, Aum Shinrikyo, a fanatical Japanese religious cult, released sarin, a deadly nerve gas, on five subway trains during Tokyo's early-morning rush hour. A male cult member boarded each of the trains carrying two or three small plastic bags covered with newspaper and, at an agreed-upon time, removed the newspaper and punctured the bags with a sharpened umbrella tip. On the trains, in the stations where they stopped, and at the station exits, people coughed, choked, experienced convulsions, and collapsed. Twelve were killed and up to five thousand injured. Had Aum succeeded in producing a purer form of the gas, the deaths could have been in the thousands or hundreds of thousands.*

---

* Robert Jay Lifton. *Destroying the World to Save It*. New York: Henry Holt, 1999, p. 3.

Shoko Asahara, leader of the terrorist group Aum Shinrikyo, appeared on a televised news program in 1995 to deny involvement in the sarin attack in the Tokyo subway. This subway gassing was one of only a few attacks in which a terrorist group used a weapon of mass destruction—in this case, a chemical weapon.

many people as possible and in as spectacular a way as possible. Recipes, or "cookbooks," for making WMD are now available on the Internet. Various groups, including al Qaeda, have conducted experiments and undertaken shopping expeditions to buy such weapons on the black market.

To date, the use of such WMD has been quite limited. Members of Aum Shinrikyo, a Japanese religious cult, sprayed sarin in a Tokyo subway in 1995 and managed to kill a dozen people. There have been a handful of other cases, including the use of anthrax spores against specific targets in the aftermath of the 9/11 attacks. The U.S. Department of Homeland Security and comparable government organizations throughout the democratic world have been preparing to prevent such WMD attacks, assuming that they are in the offing.

This may be true, but another possibility should be considered. Terrorists have been relatively conservative in their use of weapons. Bombs, guns, and knives have been their weapons of choice for more than a century. They are easy and cheap to make and easy to conceal, and they seem to work. Why change?

Another consideration is that terrorist groups may very well continue to use these highly conventional weapons but in increasingly unconventional ways. The 9/11 hijackers used box cutters that could be bought at most hardware stores to take over three commercial airliners that they then used to kill more than 3,000 people. Cell phones were used to detonate explosives placed on board commuter trains in Madrid on March 11, 2004. Hundreds died as a result. Those who carried out these destructive attacks used very common devices in innovative ways and managed to kill large numbers of people as a result. The future seems to hold more such attacks in store. The unconventional use of conventional weapons seems more likely than the use of WMD.

NOTES

Chapter 1
Confronting Terrorism

1. *Patterns of Global Terrorism* 1961–1982, 1993, 1995, 2001, Washington, D.C.: U.S. Department of State.
2. Title 22 of the United States Code, Section 2656f(d).
3. "Basque Fatherland and Liberty (ETA) from *Country Reports on Terrorism, 2004.* U. S. Department of State, April 2005. Available at http://library. nps.navy.mil/home/tgp/eta.htm.

Chapter 2
The Origins

4. Aristotle, *Politics*, Book V, quoted in Walter Laqueur (ed.), *Voices of Terror.* New York: Reed Press, 2004, pp. 13–14.
5. Paul Johnson, *A History of the Jews.* New York: Harper & Row, 1987, p. 122.
6. Norman Cohn, *The Pursuit of the Millennium.* New York: Oxford University Press, 1970.
7. Karl Heinzen, "Murder" in Walter Laqueur (ed.), *Voices of Terror.* New York: Reed Press, 2004, pp. 57–67.

8. Ibid.
9. Sergey Nechaev, "Catechism of the Revolutionist" in Walter Laqueur (ed.), *Voices of Terror.* New York: Reed Press, 2004, pp. 71–74.

Chapter 3
Modern Terrorism: The First Wave

10. Barbara Tuchman, *The Proud Tower.* New York: Macmillan, 1967, p. 73.

Chapter 4
Anticolonialism and Nationalism: The Second Wave

11. Robert Taber, *The War of the Flea.* New York: L. Stuart, 1965.

Chapter 6
The New Terrorism: The Fourth Wave

12. Brian Jenkins, "International Terrorism: A New Mode of Conflict" in David Carlton and Carlo Schaerf (eds.), *International Terrorism and World Security.* London: Croom Helm, 1975, pp. 13–49.

Badey, Thomas (ed.). *Violence and Terrorism 05/06*. Dubuque, IA: McGraw-Hill/Dushkin, 2005.

Benjamin, Daniel, and Steven Simon. *The Age of Sacred Terror*. New York: Random House, 2003.

Bergen, Peter. *Holy War Inc*. New York: The Free Press, 2001.

Coogan, Tim Pat. *The IRA*. New York: Palgrave, 2002.

Crenshaw, Martha (ed.). *Terrorism in Context*. University Park, PA: Pennsylvania State University Press, 1995.

Esposito, John. *Unholy War*. New York: Oxford University Press, 2002.

Hoffman, Bruce. *Inside Terrorism*. New York: Columbia University Press, 1999.

Laqueur, Walter (ed.). *The Terrorism Reader*. New York: New American Library, 1978.

Lewis, Bernard. *The Crisis of Islam*. New York: Modern Library, 2003.

Miller, Judith, Stephen Engleberg, and William Broad. *Germs: Biological Weapons and America's Secret War*. New York: Simon and Schuster, 2001.

The 9/11 Commission Report: Final Report of the National Commission on Terrorist Attacks Upon the United States. New York: W.W. Norton, 2004.

Rapoport, David. "Fear and Trembling: Terrorism in Three Religious Traditions." *American Political Science Review* 78 (1984): pp. 658–677.

Sageman, Marc. *Understanding Terror Networks*. Philadelphia: University of Pennsylvania Press, 2004.

Stern, Jessica. *Terror in the Name of God*. New York: HarperCollins, 2003.

Stern, Jessica. *The Ultimate Terrorists*. Cambridge, MA: Harvard University Press, 1999.

Tuchman, Barbara. *The Proud Tower*. New York: Macmillan, 1967.

Wright, Robin. *Sacred Terror: The Wrath of Militant Islam*. New York: Simon & Schuster, 1986.

BOOKS

Bergen, Peter. *Holy War Inc.* New York: The Free Press, 2001.

Ganor, Boaz. *The Counter-Terrorism Puzzle.* New Brunswick, NJ: Transaction, 2005.

Gurr, Nadine, and Benjamin Cole. *The New Face of Terrorism.* New York: I.B. Tauris, 2002.

Hewitt, Christopher. *Understanding Terrorism in America.* New York: Routledge, 2003.

Juergensmeyer, Mark. *Terror in the Mind of God.* Berkeley, CA: University of California Press, 2001.

Laqueur, Walter. *A History of Terrorism.* New Brunswick, NJ: Transaction, 2001.

Laqueur, Walter (ed.). *Voices of Terror.* New York: Reed Press, 2004.

Lewis, Bernard. *The Crisis of Islam.* New York: Modern Library, 2003.

Miller, Judith, Stephen Engleberg, and William Broad. *Germs: Biological Weapons and America's Secret War.* New York: Simon and Schuster, 2001.

The 9/11 Commission Report: Final Report of the National Commission on Terrorist Attacks Upon the United States. New York: W.W. Norton, 2004.

White, Jonathan. *Terrorism: An Introduction.* New York: Thompson-Wadsworth, 2003.

WEBSITES

The Institute for Counter-Terrorism
http://www.ict.org.il/

The National Memorial Institute for the Prevention of Terrorism
http://mipt.org/

The Terrorism Research Center
http://www.terrorism.org/

LEONARD WEINBERG is Foundation Professor of Political Science at the University of Nevada. Over the course of his career, he has been a Fulbright senior research fellow for Italy, a visiting fellow at the National Security Studies Center (University of Haifa), a visiting scholar at UCLA, a guest professor at the University of Florence, and the recipient of an H. F. Guggenheim Foundation grant for the study of political violence. He has also served as a consultant to the United Nations Office for the Prevention of Terrorism (Agency for Crime Control and Drug Prevention).

For his work in promoting Christian–Jewish reconciliation, Professor Weinberg was a recipient of the 1999 Thornton Peace Prize. His books include *Global Terrorism* (2005), *Political Parties and Terrorist Groups* (2003, with Ami Pedahzur), *Right-Wing Extremism in the Twenty-First Century* (2003, eds. with Peter Merkl), *Religious Fundamentalism and Political Extremism* (2003, eds. with Ami Pedahzur), *The Democratic Experience and Political Violence* (2001, eds. with David Rapoport), and *The Emergence of a Euro-American Radical Right* (1998, with Jeffrey Kaplan). His articles have appeared in such journals as the *British Journal of Political Science*, *Comparative Politics*, and *Party Politics*. He is the senior editor of the journal *Democracy and Security*.

WILLIAM L. EUBANK is a graduate of the University of Houston, where he earned two degrees (B.S. and M.A.) in political science. He received his Ph.D. from the University of Oregon in 1978. Before coming to the University of Nevada, he taught briefly at California State University–Sonoma and Washington State University. While at the University of Nevada, he has taught undergraduate courses in Constitutional Law, Civil Rights & Liberties, Political Parties and Elections, and graduate seminars in American Politics, the History of Political Science and Research Methods.

The author or co-author of articles and papers in areas as diverse as statistics, research design, voting, and baseball, among other subjects, he has been interested in how political violence and terrorism function as markers for political problems confronting governments. These interests have included the effect of violence on elections, stability of governmental forms, and the connection between international political violence/terror and liberal democracies. Professor Eubank is currently pursuing a project with Professor Weinberg on the "cost" of terrorism, to see if civil liberties are eroded in those countries undergoing terrorist campaigns.